RIDING
AHEAD OF THE HERD
SEI Strategic Advisor Council National Meeting

Dallas, TX / May 5-7, 2013

All the best referrals!

Stephen Wershing

SEI | New ways.
New answers.®

STOP
ASKING FOR
REFERRALS

STOP
ASKING FOR
REFERRALS

A Revolutionary New Strategy for Building a Financial Service Business That Sells Itself

STEPHEN WERSHING, CFP®

New York   Chicago   San Francisco   Lisbon   London
Madrid   Mexico City   Milan   New Delhi   San Juan
Seoul   Singapore   Sydney   Toronto

The McGraw·Hill Companies

1 2 3 4 5 6 7 8 9 0   DOC/DOC   1 0 9 8 7 6 5 4 3 2

ISBN: 978-0-07-180819-4
MHID: 0-07-180819-1

e-ISBN: 978-0-07-180820-0
e-MHID: 0-07-180820-5

McGraw-Hill books are available at special quantity discounts to use as premiums and sales promotions, or for use in corporate training programs. To contact a representative, please e-mail us at bulksales@mcgraw-hill.com.

This book is printed on acid-free paper.

The recommendations in this book are of a general nature. Be sure to check with your compliance department before taking action on any of the strategies described.

To my wife, Gaelen McCormick, who gave me the space to dedicate time to writing, provides me constant encouragement and inspiration, and is always ready to cater to my bassist desires.

CONTENTS

FOREWORD

In the financial planning/investment advisory profession, marketing is the black hole. Planners who embrace the fiduciary standard—my clients' interests always come first—tend to underemphasize marketing because it takes away from their client activities. If they *do* market, they discover that they've been given a lot of outmoded tools from the so-called experts—seminar marketing, cold calls, e-mail blasts, direct mail, asking clients to give you referrals if you did a good job for them, and so on. You could realistically conclude that the marketing activities most prevalent in our business are ineffective at best and at worst may represent a violation of the fiduciary ethos.

And yet what small business can succeed if it does no marketing?

Over the past 20 years, as a commentator and writer in the financial planning/registered investment advisor (RIA) world, I've looked at virtually all the marketing programs that advisors are exposed to. I attend 10 or 12 conferences a year and routinely go to the marketing breakout sessions. Usually I find a nugget or two that I can report back to my readers, including tips on how to use social media more effectively, or branding ideas, or suggestions on how to construct a good brochure that describes your practice. But mostly I've been disappointed.

As a connoisseur of great resources for advisors, I can (and routinely do) recommend a number of really good practice-management books and consultants, terrific tools and out-source services to save time and effort, and any number of astute resources on investments, portfolio management, and economic trends. But I haven't found a marketing resource that I could recommend wholeheartedly to advisors who want to build their practices.

Until now.

In *Stop Asking for Referrals*, Steve Wershing accomplishes several things at once. First, he helps you to deprogram your-self from the outmoded marketing ideas that you knew, instinc-tively, were ineffective and uncomfortable for clients. Instead, he focuses his full attention on referral marketing, which we all know is where virtually all new clients come from. You get sys-tematic advice on how and why to define a target market niche (which I think is also excellent practice-management advice), how to communicate your services effectively, different ways to burn that message into the minds of your clients (for the first time, I understand the origins of the term *brand*), and how to harness the natural, normal social interactions of your clients to serve your marketing efforts—all without intruding on their lives or making them feel uncomfortable.

In fact (you'll have to read the book to believe this), when you help your clients market your services, you're also enhanc-ing their status with their social peers. This is a win-win situ-ation that will feel comfortable to even the strictest, most fiduciary-oriented advisor.

You'll also learn how to get your clients to help you define your business, create your service package, and bring in business—and once again, *they* feel like *you* benefited them. You'll read about the powerful idea of social currency, the positive side of a "bad" referral, which people around you are most likely to do favors for you, and how to structure joint projects with centers of influence—and perhaps most important, the book will resolve the conflicts and hesitancies you have about marketing your practice.

I happen to believe that your services provide significant—even life-changing—benefits to the people with whom you work and that the world is better served when you begin to attract more clients. When advisors ask me how they should market their practices, I'm going to recommend this book. I hope you'll accept my recommendation as well.

Bob Veres
Inside Information

ACKNOWLEDGMENTS

This book and the fascinating journey that led to it are the products of the guidance, support, and encouragement of people I am fortunate to have helping me professionally and am grateful to have as friends.

Bruce Peters has been a friend and mentor for over 20 years. As a coach, he has helped me recognize what about me needed improvement. As a business associate, he helped me get started as a consultant, teaching me many of the finer points of organizing and facilitating client advisory boards. As a friend, he has always been available as a sounding board and a shoulder to cry on.

I have been a fan of Bob Veres for a long time. I have learned a lot from his insights on the business in his articles, books, and his newsletter, *Inside Information*. As I began consulting I brought my original idea to Bob. He told me the idea was too narrow and limiting given my skill set and that I could offer a lot more. His comments led me to discover much more exciting ideas and the path I am on now. He has also been generous in sharing his excitement for those ideas with his community of readers.

Syd LeBlanc is a dear friend and was the first editor of this manuscript. I appreciate her encouragement, guidance in what it takes to write a book, and her patient correction of all my writing mistakes, especially my utterly inconsistent use of contractions. I am deeply indebted to her for introducing me to McGraw-Hill.

Andrew Gluck has been a friend and resource for many years. He offered me a platform to promote my ideas in the advisor community. He has introduced me to people in the industry who have provided invaluable assistance. I am grateful for all his help and for the generous hospitality he and his delightful wife Mindy extend to me.

Finally, sincere thanks to the hundreds of financial professionals I have had the good fortune to work with. It is through them that I learned what it means to be a great advisor.

CHAPTER 1

WHY YOU NEED TO STOP ASKING FOR REFERRALS

It is widely understood that referrals are the best way to acquire new clients. We are told, therefore, that to build a more successful practice, we have to master the art of asking for referrals. Rubbish.

The way you have been told to attract referrals is based on an assumption that's wrong, and it is undermining your business and your relationships.

I have 23 years of experience in the investment advisor business. I have tried all the tricks.

"Who do you know that can use the kinds of services I have provided to you?"

"Can you think of three people who could use the kind of solutions I have provided to you?"

"Who else at work is going to receive an early-retirement offer like the one you just received?"

"I get paid three ways. . . ."

"Can we agree that if I do a good job, you will recommend me to other people you know?"

"The most important way I get new clients is referrals from existing clients."

"Getting new clients by referral enables me to focus more of my day on you."

I got names. I got clients. But it was always uncomfortable—for me and, more important, for my client. And the prospects I got this way were rarely the ones I most wanted and who became my best clients. Maybe I wasn't doing it right. Funny thing, though, there were times when I received a phone call, out of the blue, from a client who wanted me to call someone he knew or from a friend of a client wanting to retain me. And some of those people became great clients.

Fourteen years ago, I moved into the role of broker-dealer executive. Since then, I have worked with hundreds of financial advisors. To my relief, I found that I was not alone in my experience of asking for referrals. To my frustration, I realized that most of what is written about getting referrals is wrong. Yes, referrals are the lifeblood of most successful practices. And asking is a lousy way to get them. To perfect your skill at asking for referrals is to master a crude, outdated tool. It is the equivalent of becoming an expert in writing with a quill. I wanted a word processor.

If you work hard at being more effective at asking for referrals, will you get more? Yep. If you get more expert at sharpening and using your quill, will you be able to write more than if you did not? Sure. Will you ever come close to the speed and power of the most rudimentary typewriter? Not in a million years!

If you make more cold calls, will you get more clients? You bet. Is cold calling at the center of your marketing plan? Has it propelled you to superstardom in the advisory business? If so, congratulations. Now put down this book and get back on the phone—you don't need this information. You can succeed just fine without it.

THE NEW COLD CALLING

For the rest of us, we have moved on to more sophisticated and effective means of marketing. When I got into the business, cold calling was just being eclipsed as the state of the art in client acquisition. I was receiving direct mail from Steve Anderson, the "Cold Call Cowboy," into the 1990s. But the company I started with was pioneering a new client-acquisition strategy—seminars. It was powerful. I could call human resources directors at companies in town and go into the company at lunchtime and present financial planning concepts to the employees. I remember carrying around those overhead transparencies—I didn't use a personal computer in my practice until 1989, and I don't think I owned a copy of PowerPoint until the mid-1990s.

As seminars grew more popular, they got overdone and abused. Financial salespeople used seminars as an opportunity to sell from the podium. Eventually, corporate seminars became more difficult to get. And dinner seminars became populated more and more by people more interested in the dinner than in the information. We learned to network.

There were networking events, and there was *power networking*. Then it was the Internet and having a website for your practice. Now it is social media. And through all of that, the art and science of attracting referrals stayed pretty much unchanged.

Asking for referrals is the cold calling of referral marketing strategy. Like cold calling, it will work (to an extent) if you do it consistently. And as with cold calling, you run the risk of turning off as many people as you attract by doing it. However, unlike with cold calling, there is a cost to turning people off by asking for referrals. If you cold-call someone and give her a bad impression, chances are that she doesn't know you, and it won't hurt you if she ends up feeling uncomfortable because of how you approached her. When you ask for referrals, the person you risk making uncomfortable is someone with whom you want to continue having a relationship, someone you want to have a high opinion of you—your client. What is it they say about puppies? Don't poop where you eat.

What have you been encouraged to say? "Referrals are part of how I get paid." You mean I'm not paying you enough? Could I pay you a little more and not have to start handing over my personal relationships? "Referrals help both of us because with them I can spend less time marketing and more time on client service." So if I can't come up with enough names, the service you provide me will suffer? The worst thing about these approaches to referrals is that they focus on you and not on your client. Ideally, everything you do with your clients, except perhaps sending them an invoice, should focus on benefits to them.

Here are some of the problems created by constantly asking your clients for referrals:

- **It places demands on clients.** Your relationships with clients are not like your relationships with friends. In a friendship, you do each other favors because you like each other and are important to each other. While most advisors count friends among their clients, the fundamental relationship is for you to provide a service to clients and for them to compensate you for it. (We will get to the whole compensation thing in just a minute.) Asking your clients to serve you gets the relationship backward.

- *It violates client expectations.* When clients retain an advisor, they are looking to receive services, and in return, they are willing to pay. Everyone understands that relationship. When you begin asking for more than simple payment, you run a significant risk of surprising your client with an expectation from the relationship he had not counted on. Surprises like that are generally not positive experiences for the client.

- *It converts referrals into transactions.* Many training programs recommend framing the referral request as an exchange. "If we do this, we would like you to do that." This establishes a weak basis for a referral. Ideally, clients refer to us because they are thrilled with the experience and want to share that with people they care about. Reducing it to an economic transaction cheapens it. Giving us a referral can be a very positive experience for our clients. But, as with any other activity we enjoy doing, doing it as a business transaction takes most of the fun out of it.

- *It distorts the message you want to communicate.* Many programs recommend introducing the idea of referrals with such phrases as, "It is part of how I get paid" or "If you help me find new clients, I can spend less time marketing and more time providing service to you." Most of these approaches confuse the client. "I'm not paying you enough? So you're spending all your time marketing and not taking care of me?" There is tremendous opportunity to confuse the client about how you run your business.

- *The biggest problem of all is that it puts the focus on you.* In your relationship, the focus should be on the client. In a well-designed referral system, the focus remains on the client. Clients provide referrals because they derive benefits from introducing their friends and acquaintances, not because it is an obligation. Once the activity changes to providing you benefits, you have just short-circuited much of the motivation for providing them to you.

HIJACKING THE PROCESS

We don't get more referrals just because we ask for them. No less an authority than financial advisor marketing expert Bill Good recognizes this, and he refuses to allow his salespeople to ask for referrals. As he puts it, "They manifestly do not work."[1] In fact, Good tells the story of an advisor who got a pesky client to stop calling him by asking for a referral each time she called![2] Asking is a means of attempting to hijack the process. We don't have respect for the process, and we don't have patience for the process to play itself out. What we want is the instant gratification of the results without allowing the natural process to happen. We want to jump directly to the end and get the benefit rather than facilitate the natural way that it happens.

It's a little like Russell Crowe playing the role of John Nash in *A Beautiful Mind*. In the movie, his friends bring him to a bar and find a single girl at the bar. They finally persuade him to go up to the girl and ask her out. He doesn't know how to ask a girl for a date, so he just goes for the gold. Here is what he says: "I don't exactly know what I am required to say in order for you to have intercourse with me, so could we just assume I said all that? I mean, essentially what we are talking about here is fluid exchange. We could just skip straight to the sex."

How do you suppose that scene turned out? Not well for Nash. She wouldn't want to go to bed with him just because it was good for him. Besides not having any interest in him, there are real risks involved for her. He doesn't appreciate that for her to want to go to bed with him, she needs to have certain feelings about him.

When clients make a referral to us, it is because they feel certain things about us. They must feel strongly enough about what they will get out of it for it to be worth the risk they expose themselves to by sharing a friend with us. Making a referral must be an experience the client benefits from. And if you attempt to disrespect your client and go directly for the result without having respect for the process that goes with it, you'll get metaphorically slapped, just like Nash did.

Let me give you an example from outside of our business about what's wrong with the process. Let's say that you go to a restaurant, you have a fabulous time, you have a wonderful evening, and you meet a friend of yours the next day who asks, "I would like to take my wife out to dinner tonight, and we would like to try someplace new. Is there any place you could recommend?" What will you say? Well, of course, you will tell him the story about what a wonderful time you had at the restaurant last night. And how will you feel about it? You will feel good. You're helping your friend have a good time. You're giving your friend something of value. You're showing him that you're an expert in a small way in an area that's meaningful to him.

Now let's replay this in a format that should be more familiar to you as a financial advisor. You go out to a restaurant, you have a fabulous time. You have a wonderful evening. And with the check the waiter brings a piece of paper and a pen and says, "Along with your paying the bill, I would like to get the names of five of your friends who dine out periodically and their phone numbers." How would you feel about that? Well, if you're like most of the people who come to my programs, you would feel a little bit strange. You would feel uncomfortable. Why? Because that process was all about the needs of the restaurant and not about all the benefits you can get from recommending the restaurant to your friends. It violates the social contract you have with the restaurant. It reflects a fundamental misunderstanding of why people refer their friends to restaurants they enjoy.

Bill Good had an even better example. Suppose that you go to the doctor's office to be treated for something. At the end of the appointment, the doctor asks, "Do you know anyone with a similar disease who could use my service?"[3]

PROSPECTS NEED TO FIND YOU AT THE RIGHT TIME

Asking for referrals is also ineffective because we are in an event-driven business. And when we ask for referrals, we won't meet the prospects when they need us.

Clients typically seek out an advisor because something has happened or changed. Very few people wake up in the morning and say to themselves, "I think I will find a new financial advisor today." It happens, and sometimes a change of attitude can be the trigger. But most often it's because a situation arises that requires that a client find advice.

I was reminded of this the other day when I was working with an advisor on his value proposition. Like so many advisors, he told me that he works with clients who are "in transition." We may be in an event-driven business partly because we have designed it that way: money in motion, life-changing circumstances, retirement distributions, sudden money. So many of the things we tell people we specialize in involve an event.

Regardless of where they come from, it is clear that good referrals are defined partly by being introduced at the right time for the prospect. And the probability that the time you ask your client for a referral will turn out to be just right for the prospect is minuscule. Odds are that if you ask for referrals, you will be calling those prospects at a time when they are just not receptive to your message. I think of it this way: From the prospect's perspective, you are like a great plumber who shows up unannounced and unexpected on someone's doorstep. If a plumber came to visit you out of the blue, would you hire him? Right then?

Getting referrals by asking is not evidence of the supremacy of the method but a testament to Abraham Maslow, a founder of humanistic psychology, who famously said, "It is tempting, if the only tool you have is a hammer, to treat everything as if it were a nail."[4] If the only way you know how to acquire clients is to ask, then you will "prove" that it's the best method.

WE DON'T GET REFERRALS BECAUSE WE ASK

However, asking for referrals is not the best method. Through my own experience and my work with advisors, I knew that asking was not effective. The advisors I worked with knew. Even if they wanted to believe it was the best way, most had difficulty sticking with it because it is uncomfortable and unnatural. It is time we pulled the art of attracting referrals out of the cold-calling era. We now have a more sophisticated approach.

In the past year, a book and a study were published that gave me insight into finding a better way. The study was "Anatomy of the Referral" by Julie Littlechild.[5] In her survey of clients of financial advisors, she discovered that practically everyone who answered the question indicated that they were responding to the need of a friend. And, essentially, no one reported that it was because their advisor asked for it. This proved to me that asking is not the natural way referrals happen.

The book was *The Referral Engine*, by John Jantsch.[6] In it, Jantsch lays out how referrals happen, why we refer, and a host of ideas on how to stimulate referrals. With these ideas in hand, I did a lot more research on strategies that proved effective in attracting referrals. I incorporated these ideas into my work with financial advisors. The book you are holding is the product of what I have learned and what I have helped advisors to put into action.

In her studies "The Economics of Loyalty" and "Anatomy of the Referral," Julie Littlechild demonstrates that receiving referrals from clients has little statistical relationship to how or how often clients are asked. There is simply no clear straight line between asking clients for referrals the way we have been traditionally trained to do it and the best referrals you actually receive.

In her survey of more than 1,000 clients who use financial advisors, one of the questions Littlechild asked was, "What were the circumstances of the last referral you gave to your advisor?"

Half of the people said that they were asked specifically by a friend to recommend a financial advisor. Over half the people communicated some financial need for which the person knew his financial advisor had a solution. And how many people said that the circumstance of their last referral was that the advisor asked for it? Two percent, which is statistically equivalent to zero. Essentially no one gave a referral because the advisor asked for it. They gave a referral because their friend expressed a need, and they wanted to help (Figure 1.1).

Most referral programs reflect a hunter mentality. We must go out and stalk and capture the referral. How do you suppose the prey feels in this relationship?

The new research indicates that you can attract referrals without having to demand them. You probably have seen examples of this in your own experience. Do you know anyone who gets referrals and never asks? Some advisory practices actually have a policy of not asking.[7] Under the hunter mental-

Figure 1.1   Reasons for making a referral.

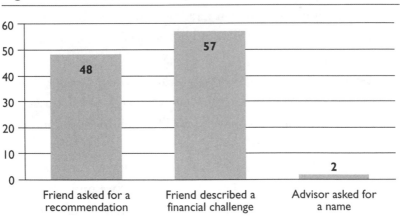

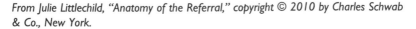

From Julie Littlechild, "Anatomy of the Referral," copyright © 2010 by Charles Schwab & Co., New York.

ity, this would be impossible. Animals don't just wander up to you and say, "Here, stick the spear in me."

I prefer to think of referrals from the perspective of a farmer rather than from that of a hunter. Under the farmer model, you prepare the soil, plant the seeds, and nurture the field. A crop will grow.

I keep hearing in referral training programs how important it is not to release the process to clients. If you want dependable, consistent referrals, you need to be in control. The farmer does not approach it this way. Could you imagine a farmer being obsessed with the progress of every seed? He knows that if he plants enough seeds in fertile soil and carefully tends to the field, he will get a good crop. Not every seed will germinate. Not every plant will thrive. But he will get ample yield.

Prepare a fertile field, tend to your crops, and you will have a bountiful harvest.

Am I actually advocating never asking for referrals? Not really, although many businesses get consistent referrals without asking directly. If you ask, do it the right way. Dan Richards and John Jantsch have both written about creating referral systems focused on asking for referrals in a way that benefits the clients.

What we need is for clients to recall us when the opportunity to refer arises—and to mention us. We can build a strategy to help increase the odds that this will happen at those moments of truth. We can pursue a strategy to generate referrals without being in constant control of each referral, made when the time is right, for reasons that benefit the client if we understand the principles. In order to do this, we first need to understand how referrals happen.

CHAPTER 2

HOW AND WHY REFERRALS HAPPEN

If you struggle with attracting referrals, there's a good chance that part of the reason is because you don't understand how and why referrals happen. If that's the case, you're not alone. The biggest problem financial advisors face with regard to referrals is the widespread ignorance of and lack of attention paid to the process that gives rise to referrals. Once you understand the circumstances that surround referrals and appreciate the reasons why people give them, it becomes much easier to develop a plan that enhances that natural process. What most advisors attempt to do is ignore the process and simply ask for the results.

SOCIAL CURRENCY

People are social animals. As human beings, we have a natural need to refer. We do it all the time and for all kinds of reasons.

A very long time ago, a referral could have saved your life. A good tip on where to find the game or fish that day could have meant the difference between eating (and living) or not. Of course, we've progressed a long way from there, but referrals are still important to us as a society. They are social currency. They are a way of expanding influence. They are a way of networking. It is perfectly natural to want to do things for the people who are important to us, and providing referrals is one way we can. Being the source of good information and a person other people look to for advice also makes us feel important.

Most of us are referring all the time. As financial advisors, we don't get more referrals mainly because we get the process wrong. And the reason we get the process wrong is because we don't understand how referrals happen and what the process is about.

As John Jantsch says in his book, *The Referral Engine: Teaching Your Business to Market Itself,* "Being recognized as a source of good information, including referrals, is a great way to connect with others. Think about how eagerly you responded the last time someone asked you for directions, offering up your favorite shortcut and tips for avoiding traffic. We all do it. Making referrals is a deeply satisfying way to connect with others, and asking for referrals is just the other side of the same phenomenon. I think the growth of many popular social networks can be traced to the fact that people love to connect and form communities around shared ideas."[1]

In his book, *The New Art and Science of Referral Marketing,* Scott Degraffenreid used social network analysis to examine why people make referrals. His study demonstrated something that makes intuitive sense—people refer to elevate their standing with their peers.[2]

Try this thought experiment. Who or what have you referred recently? Have your friends or business associates asked for recommendations of products or service providers? Have you told anyone about a new song, a movie you have seen recently, or a restaurant you have just gone to for the first time? What were the circumstances that led you to talk about those experiences? How did they happen? Why did you do it? How did you feel about doing it?

Have you asked to be referred to someone or some company lately? I mean, have you asked a friend or acquaintance to make a recommendation to you for something you needed to solve or wanted to experience? Did you need a contractor, an attorney, or a landscaper? Did you want to try a new restaurant?

I know I am making referrals all the time, although I usually would call them suggestions or recommendations. Here are a few that I have made recently or make fairly regularly:

- Since I work with financial advisors, I will often get questions about tools and resources. I frequently suggest mutual funds or families. I am happy to recommend the client relationship-management system I use, Redtail.

- A client of my retail practice needed some short-term financing, and I was happy to recommend and coordinate a loan through a regional bank.

- I love the software applications Evernote and Nozbe. As a busy consultant and executive who struggles with attention-deficit disorder (ADD), I have found that these programs improve my life.

- I am a fan of Mark Sisson and *The Primal Blueprint.*[3] If I get into a conversation with someone about diet or health, I will frequently direct them to Mark's book or website.

- I recommend my auto mechanic pretty regularly. There have been many times when he has directed me back to the dealership because he believed that my problem was covered under warranty. Other times he has talked me out of repairs on a beat-up Jeep or van I used to own to carry things around for home-improvement projects because they were too expensive relative to the value of the vehicle. I believe that he won't charge me to do something unless it's necessary.

- I encourage at least a few people a year to become members of the country club where I am a member.

- My wife and I love food and wine and frequently talk about local restaurants and vineyards in the Finger Lakes Region of New York where we live.

Once you reflect on it, you will likely realize that you make referrals pretty regularly. Your clients do, too. They likely refer people to you more than you realize. In her study, "Anatomy of the Referral,"[4] Julie Littlechild found that 91 percent of clients were comfortable providing a referral to their financial advisor, and 29 percent had made a referral. One of the primary questions she hoped to shed light on was why, when such a large majority of clients are comfortable providing referrals, "only" 29 percent actually did. It's a good question, and she uncovered some answers I will address later on. In addition, I am intrigued by the 29 percent. Most of the advisors I know would be thrilled to receive referrals from almost a third of their client base. What portion of your client base do you think referred someone to you in the last year? If you asked, I bet a much larger proportion would tell you that they did. We will get back to this statistic in a little while. For now, let's take a look at whether clients feel comfortable making a referral to you and why they would.

I specifically say "make a referral to you" and not "give you a referral" because when it happens naturally, a referral is not something a client gives you; a referral is something she gives a friend. If you go back to Figure 1.1, you will see that the top two reasons for offering a referral are because a friend asked for a referral and because a friend expressed a financial challenge. Your client is telling her friend about you not because she wants to benefit you but because she wants to benefit the friend and to benefit herself.

Did you try the thought experiment I described earlier? Who have you recommended to friends over the past month? Why did you do it? Why do I tell people about my auto mechanic, or those software applications, or Mark Sisson? My mechanic does not pay me to tell people about him; he provides me no incentive to recommend him—no discounts or coupons or certificates for a steak dinner if I send three people his way. And I assure you that Mark Sisson does not even know that I exist, much less that I am a fan. I encourage friends to patronize those businesses because I care about them, my friends. I do it because I want them to have a better experience taking care of their car, because I want them to avoid getting ripped off, and because I want them to be healthier. And I want them to think better of me for having turned them on to something that was useful to them. That is why we naturally make referrals.

Thus, if people want to realize the benefits of providing a referral (e.g., obtain social currency, expand influence, etc.) and can accomplish that by directing a friend to you because they believe that you will help that friend solve a problem, they will refer people to you. Attracting referrals, then, becomes largely a matter of training clients to remember to mention you at the right time. It's all about helping people to remember you when *they* can benefit from mentioning you. It's not about giving you names when you ask; it's about remembering to refer you when the opportunity arises, so you have to prepare clients for the opportunity to refer. "Who can you think of that could use my services?" is about asking your client to help you. "I know someone who can help you solve that problem" is about a client helping a friend.

Thinking about it another way, when you ask for a referral, you're essentially asking your clients to sell for you. And that's not the role they signed up for. Consider it in your own experience. Is there a professional with whom you work or whose services you have used who you would happily refer anytime someone expressed a need—a car mechanic, a plumber, a lawyer? Most of us have at least one or two people we deal with on a regular basis who we would be thrilled to refer. Let me ask you this, Who will you call about that person today? Well, of course, you're not going to wake up and ask yourself, "Who can I call to tell about this great plumber I know?" That's not how it works. How many clients will you commit to attracting for those people this year? None, of course—that's not why you recommend them. You do it because it benefits *you*, not the person to whom you are referring someone.

"GIVING" YOU REFERRALS

Now, in addition to making referrals to you, clients occasionally will give you referrals. That is, they will offer you the contact information of a friend of theirs without the friend asking for it. The concept of expanding influence and creating social currency applies to a client's relationship with you just as it does to the client's relationships with his friends. Clients want to help you, they want you to think highly of them, and they want to be seen by you as a resource. They want to make deposits in your psychic bank, just as they want to make deposits into their accounts with their friends. We make referrals to help our friends who are in business, just as we make referrals to friends who need a problem solved. If I have a friend in the mortgage banking business and someone else indicates to me that he might be buying a home or thinking about refinancing, there is a good chance I will send that person to my friend. As long as my friend does a workmanlike job at writing mortgages, I want to help her build her business.

For example, my business coach is also a good friend of mine. Sometimes when we meet, I might give him the contact information of someone else I know, along with the suggestion that he contact that person. That other person may not have told me that he was looking for coaching services or necessarily expressed a need that would be satisfied by my friend's coaching, but I want my friend to succeed, and I want to help him to build his business.

Many of us have clients who have become our friends as well. They want to help us build our business, to help us succeed, so they give us referrals. Frequently they will do so without our asking for them.

Julie Littlechild's study, "Anatomy of the Referral"[5] shows us the role of this desire. Although most participants in her study made referrals in response to a friend's request for a recommendation or expression of a financial need, the motivation for providing the referral was most frequently the desire to reciprocate for the advisor's doing a good job. In response to the question, "Which of the following best describes the motivation behind providing a referral to your advisor?" 58 percent of respondents answered, "My advisor has done a good job for me, and I wanted to return the favor by helping him or her build the business." While this desire, as the study notes, is not enough to provide a meaningful stream of referrals, it does provide a motivation to give them. Do a good enough job for your clients, and they will want to help you in return. In fact, to some extent, clients perceive helping you as a way to protect their own well-being.

Whether personal friends or not, we enjoy a special relationship with our clients. There is a unique dynamic between a client and his or her financial advisor. To some extent, clients associate our success with their own. Many of them feel that for them to do well financially, we need to do well financially. It could be that they feel subconsciously that if we succeed, they will succeed, that the better we do, the better they will do. Alternatively, it could be that our success is just a prerequisite for theirs; for them to succeed, we need to succeed. Either way, I have seen that particular dynamic play out and have heard it from advisors I have worked with.

Bruce Peters, whose company, CABHQ, was a pioneer in organizing client advisory boards for financial advisors (and who taught me many of the finer points of doing advisory boards and with whom I continue to work), noticed this the first time he conducted an advisory board meeting for a financial advisor. After having done hundreds of advisory board meetings, he was amazed at the level of engagement of the participants in the meeting. Everyone was invested in the process—much more deeply than in practically any meeting he had done before. As he watched the dynamic of the meeting and reflected on it, he had what he calls "a blinding flash of the obvious." Of course everyone would be invested in the process, he realized. They all have a vested interest in the advisor's success.

So clients will give you referrals to reward you for a job well done and because they like you personally and want you to succeed. This is one natural process you can encourage without putting clients on the spot and compromising your relationships with them as the "Who do you know?" question will do. Reminding them that the most significant way your business grows is through your clients referring prospective clients can help to enhance this type of referral. But there are vastly more rewards to be gained by facilitating the natural opportunities for clients to make a referral when they are not with you but with other people.

BE REFERABLE

Therefore, beyond your clients' desire to help you, how can you enhance the natural process of a referral happening? First, you have to be worth talking about.

Marketing guru Seth Godin, in an interview for the Duct Tape Marketing podcast, said, "If the marketplace isn't talking about you, there's a reason. The reason is that you're boring."[6] Do you deliver an experience people *want* to pass along?

Although delivering a superior client experience is not enough to attract consistent referrals, it is a prerequisite. How much do you do to demonstrate that you are the best financial advisor to handle your clients' particular problems? Part of that is niche marketing, and we will get to that in a subsequent chapter. Another part of it is being conspicuous about that niche—writing articles, publishing a blog, sponsoring events, and taking specialized training all focused on the specific kinds of client issues you work on.

Referral consultant Paul McCord says, "The traditional method of 'do a good job and ask for referrals' does not give your client a reason to give you referrals. We make the assumption that if we have done a good job, the client will like and respect us and be willing to give us referrals. Again, this is far from the case. Most clients will not give good, quality referrals just because they like you or because you have done a good job for them. You must give them a reason to give you referrals. They need to understand why it is in their best interest to give you referrals."[7]

If your clients understand how they can contribute to a friend's well-being by connecting that friend with you, you will find that happening more often. If they know that you can solve their friend's need because of your services, because of your knowledge and experience about that need, and because you deliver a consistent and high-quality experience, then they will make a referral because they will benefit by introducing you. They will provide their friend with a solution, they will make a deposit in their psychic bank account with that friend, and they will boost their credibility all by connecting their friend to you. If you make it easy to refer you, you will get more referrals. If referring you increases your clients' stature

among their friends who are in your target market, you will
receive more referrals.

THE TWO TIMES CLIENTS REFER

Apart from when clients are meeting with you, there are two
times people will think to refer you—and no, when you ask is
not one of them. The two times are just after they have a positive experience with you and when a friend expresses a need for
a solution that you represent.

Clients will talk about you after a meeting or interaction,
provided that it's memorable. The good thing about this is that
you don't have to do much to prompt it beyond giving them an
experience worth talking about. People naturally discuss with
friends what's been happening recently. If you take care to create a positive experience, you have done what you can. Have
you ever gotten an unsolicited referral from a client soon after
meeting with him? That's this effect in action. Marketers refer
to it as *top-of-mind awareness*.

After I go to my chiropractor, I probably will mention her to
a couple of people over the next few days. My back feels good.
There have been a few memorable experiences involving back
pain that she relieved. In casual conversation, there's a good
chance that I will bring them up. If anyone I meet over those
next couple of days has pain they are not talking about or has
been considering going to a chiropractor, they probably will
ask me about her, and she will get a referral.

The bad thing is that this effect does not last long. Maybe
a day or two. A longer-lasting way to stimulate referrals is
to have your clients associate you with some specific solution

or experience. The key, then, is to define what solution you represent so clearly that when a friend expresses a need to your client, you naturally pop to mind. Rather than top-of-mind awareness, which is fleeting, we want to take advantage of what psychologists call *assisted recall*. When one of your clients hears a description of the kind of problem you solve, you want it to remind them of you, causing you to spring to the top of their mind.

I recently hired a plumbing company to pump out my septic tank. This is not something I do very often. In fact, I have been in this house for almost 20 years and have not had the tank pumped once. (I know, bad idea. Like many people, I procrastinate on the preventive maintenance stuff.) But I had a remodeling project going on and needed an inspection. The inspection required that the tank be pumped. I mentioned it to people. I asked around. A friend suggested a company, and it turned out to be great.

And that's how referrals happen. If that company had called me a year ago and told me that it was an expert at pumping septic tanks, I would have replied, "Not now, thanks." (Even though I should have thought about it. But I was, I don't know, packing for vacation or cutting the lawn or something.) But now I needed one. And because my friend knew that this company was good at cleaning septic systems, he mentioned the company to me when I described my predicament.

Translate that into our business. We know that clients should be thinking about retirement, college funding, estate planning, and their other important planning issues now. But they don't. They think of them most frequently when they are forced to. They think of them when something happens that they have to deal with or that a friend or family member has to deal with. They think about whether they should take the pension or a rollover when they get their early retirement offer. They think about updating their will when a parent or friend dies and leaves a mess. They reconsider their all-technology stock portfolio when the market has dropped 5 or 10 percent. If you communicate with the public about financial-planning issues, you probably encourage people to do planning before it becomes necessary. However, because we are directing that message at human beings, many will take up the issue only when it crowds out other things competing for their attention.

We can extol the merits of maintaining the plumbing, but most people will have the septic tank pumped (at least the first time) only when they have to.

The key concept is to have your client remember you when someone she knows needs you, not when you decide you want a new client. What we must focus on is making sure that our clients understand what particular solutions we can deliver or what experiences we can provide. If we can make that easy to recall, they will remember us when they hear someone describe a need for what we do. In the end, we don't really want our clients to share with us the names of their friends. We want our clients to share our names with their friends at the right time.

More often, the opportunity to refer arises from someone expressing a need to one of your clients or centers of influence. Consider this hypothetical scenario:

Joe is unhappy with his advisor. He recently had an appointment for a portfolio review and came away from it dissatisfied. He is not happy with the performance. He doesn't understand how his advisor makes investment decisions, and his advisor does not do a great job of explaining the thought processes behind what he buys and sells. So Joe does what most people do who are thinking about a change—he asks his friends. Who do you use? Are you happy? What kinds of services do you get from your financial person? How has your experience been?

If Joe is talking to one of your clients and that client likes you and the experience he has had with you, and it sounds like what you do is a good match for what Joe is looking for, you likely will get a referral.

FIRST, CONFIRM THAT YOUR CLIENTS WOULD WANT TO REFER YOU

For this kind of scenario to materialize, one thing we need to confirm is that your clients would, in fact, refer you. The first component of clients' willingness to refer you to others is that they are happy with your service. And that bears checking. You probably assume, as do most advisors, that your clients are satisfied. Not all advisors are correct in that assumption.

In June 2011, the Institute for Private Investors released a study showing a shocking gap between how satisfied wealth managers believed their ultrahigh-net-worth clients were and how satisfied those clients said they were. In the report, "Both Sides Now,"[8] 63 percent of the clients reported being "fully satisfied" with their advisor relationship. That statistic alone should give you pause. When the advisors were asked, 95 percent of them believed that all their clients were fully satisfied.

In March 2011, Northstar Research Partners released a study[9] showing that although 51 percent of the 1,290 people they surveyed indicated that they were "highly satisfied" with their advisor and another 43 percent were "very satisfied," 36 percent of people with more than $100,000 to invest would consider moving to another firm. One-quarter of respondents would drop their advisor for another who could provide them with better investment options or a higher level of customer service.

In Julie Littlechild's studies, clients are categorized by how they demonstrate their loyalty to their advisors. The highest level, "Engaged clients," comprised only 24 percent of respondents to her survey. And that category provided *all* the referrals.

These are a few recent examples of how tenuous client loyalty can be. I see these kinds of articles pretty regularly. The practical upshot is to illustrate how dangerous it is to assume that your clients are loyal and happy and that loyalty and happiness are not enough—and that to find out how happy, loyal, and willing to refer clients they are requires that you ask.

Conducting a client survey or organizing a client advisory board, which I will discuss later, are good ways of confirming that you are delivering the kind of experience your clients want to share with other people. Make a discussion of clients' expectations a standard part of your service process so that you can ensure that you meet or exceed them.

BECOMING THE SOLUTION

We are in an event-driven business. Many more referrals are likely to be generated if our clients pick up on their friends describing events where we can be of help. Focusing on particular events also enhances the likelihood that when we receive a referral, it will be for something we want to focus our practice on—someone in our target market.

When prospective clients are in the market for a new financial advisor, they are typically either seeking the solution to a particular problem or seeking a particular experience. To enhance the natural process of referrals, you will want to become closely associated with the solution or experience you have tailored your practice to deliver. Attracting referrals then becomes the result of regularly and consistently communicating that solution or experience and the particular kind of client or client situation where it offers the most value.

How does this contrast with how you approach referrals now? If you have been taught to ask for referrals, it approaches the process exactly backward. Successfully attracting referrals depends on your clients remembering you at an opportune time. Asking for referrals requires that your clients remember specific friends and acquaintances when it is the right time for you.

To be referred on a consistent and long-term basis, you need to be easy to recall. You need to make sure that when a client's friend or acquaintance relays a need that you can satisfy, you quickly spring to mind. You need to be like a ribbon on the client's finger that reminds her to mention you when the circumstances are right. You need to own a particular spot on the client's brain. You want to take enough ownership of that particular place in the client's brain that when a friend of hers comes along and tickles that spot, your name inadvertently falls out of her mouth. You want it to be almost Pavlovian: When a client hears someone describe the kind of situation you specialize in, you want the client to mention you almost reflexively.

Now, let's get back to that 29 percent of clients I mentioned earlier who say that they have provided a referral. When I asked groups of advisors how many of them receive referrals from that many clients, practically none of them said they do. But the *clients* believe that they are giving those referrals. And they probably are giving out your name and maybe your number or website to that many people each year. This is not particularly surprising. I tell a lot of people about my car mechanic, but probably very few of them give him a call. The exciting part about that statistic is that clients are willing to offer a referral and will follow through on it when the opportunity arises. Key, then, is to understand what the right circumstances are and to provide the clients with the appropriate understanding and resources to respond. And by resources I do not mean information. It is not adequate to give your client a business card and then consider your role in enhancing referrals complete. What I mean is to offer them what they need to know so that they can achieve their own goals by providing a referral. And their goals primarily revolve around their ability to help their friends and associates.

So the question is, Why are you not receiving calls from those people that 29 percent of your clients are referring? It may be because what your clients have expressed to their friends or associates is not compelling enough to prompt a phone call or an e-mail. Getting your clients to the point that they mention you is the first step. The next step is to work with them on how to describe what you do in a way that the prospect immediately sees an easily defined value to having a conversation with you.

How do your clients describe you to other people? "My financial advisor is really good." "She listens to me." "He doesn't just want to sell me something." "I really trust her." "I have always had good experiences with him." "I like the way she has managed my portfolio." Nice praise, to be sure.

But nothing that would prompt the prospect to pull out a pen and say, "What was that number again? I need to give her a call." For that to happen, your client needs to describe more than a good experience. It would be good if it were something specific. Certainly it must be compelling. If it were timely, that would be better. Clients must understand a particular kind of solution or experience you represent. Something that is compelling to people in your target market. Something that, if the prospect is in your target market, he will recognize as something he needs or wants. Something that is different from what he is getting now and different from what he hears from other financial advisors.

For your clients to understand what your firm specializes in and who to refer to you, these things must first be clear in *your* mind. The process begins with you understanding your target market and value proposition. So let us now turn to how you can define those key ingredients to attracting referrals and what role they will play in your referral marketing plan.

CHAPTER 3

WHO'S YOUR TARGET?

This is a book about how to attract referrals. And the first step in attracting referrals is knowing who you want to attract.

Successful referral marketing means that you have a system in place that makes sure, as best as possible, that people mention you to their friends and acquaintances and persuade them (or make them feel compelled) to call you. This means that they need to know who you're looking for and why. The better they understand the kinds of clients you can offer the most value to, the more likely it is that they will mention you to that person when they meet. And in order for people to know who you're looking for, *you* need to know who you're looking for. Do you?

YOU NEED TO KNOW WHO YOU ARE LOOKING FOR

When Andrew Sullivan, of Sullivan and Schlieman in Atlanta, formed his advisory board, one of the board's top recommendations was to give each board member a card listing Sullivan's services and accomplishments. Their request was to "tell us how to sell you."

In a recent client advisory board I facilitated, the participants said to the advisor, "Tell us who your ideal client is so that we know who to refer." This is not the first time I've heard that kind of feedback from clients.

Experiences like this raise two critically important points. First, there is clearly a strong willingness, even an enthusiasm, on the part of clients to make referrals. This is not really surprising—Julie Littlechild's research[1] has shown that as many as 91 percent of our clients are willing to refer. (It also demonstrates why participants on an advisory board tend to be a firm's best referral sources!)

Second, it is the strongest proof I can imagine that advisors must clearly define what they do and for whom. They must be able to describe their niche, their target market. Remember, these advisory boards are composed of an advisor's best clients—the ones who should know best what the advisor has to offer.

YOUR CLIENTS NEED TO KNOW WHO TO REFER

While people generally refer for their own purposes, many of them want to help you if they can. But they need to know how. And helping them understand will boost the natural way referrals occur (people looking to help friends) even more than boosting their ability to send people your way because they want to help you. One of the primary reasons we do not receive more (or better) referrals is simply because our clients do not know who we want them to refer to us. Dan Allison is a consultant who discusses many of the same ideas about client feedback as I do, and his experience is similar to mine when he works with groups of advisors' clients. In an interview for AdvisorPod,[2] he relayed some basic questions he asked these groups, one of which was, "What would an ideal referral look like?"

When Allison asks this question of client focus groups, by far the most common answer is, "I don't know." And if that's the response you get, too, you will know why you aren't getting more referrals. Your clients are not sure who you're looking for. And whatever you have done so far to define and communicate your target market, your value proposition, and your ideal client, you still have work to do.

Try this experiment: Next time you talk to a couple of clients you are on particularly good terms with and who would be willing to take a minute for a little thought experiment, ask them this question: If I sent you into a cocktail party in the next room full of all kinds of people, and I asked you to refer a couple of them to me as prospective clients, how would you figure out who would be the best ones to send to me? Michael Kitces, director of Financial Planning at Pinnacle Advisory Group in Columbia, Maryland, and a well-known speaker and blogger, described the dilemma well in a blog post about wanting to refer an insurance expert to other financial advisors. He respected this expert and thought that he had a lot to offer other practitioners. But when he tried to understand the kinds of clients this consultant most wanted to work with, he ran into an obstacle. "As [the insurance expert] explained it, 'It's difficult to describe what I do and how I work with people because there are so many variations depending on exactly what my client needs that my services ultimately are customized for each of my clients.'" In the end, Kitces could not refer him at all. "It was a very problematic outcome. I wanted to refer him, but I couldn't. I didn't know what kinds of firms were the best fit for him. I just couldn't give him any referrals, even though I wanted to!"[3] Do you ever find yourself describing your ideal client the way this expert did? That can help explain why people don't send you more referrals.

RECOGNIZING TARGET PROSPECTS IN YOUR NEW CLIENT PROCESS

Which clients do you want to attract? When you are interviewing a prospect, how do you decide whether to accept him as a client? If you are like the advisors I speak with, there is surprisingly little relationship between the answers to these questions.

At a think tank I facilitated in conjunction with the Financial Planning Association's (FPA) conference Business Solutions 2011, I asked both questions. In response to the target-market question, I got pretty much the answers I was expecting—prospects described in terms of demographics, income level, profession, or investable assets. Julie Littlechild, who brought me in to facilitate the meeting, then wanted to know whether these target characteristics appeared in questions during an initial interview. Did the advisors use checklists or similar devices with prospective clients? Did they stick to their own standards? Once they had established what an "A" client was, were they consistent in accepting only "A's"?

Then I asked the advisors about their client onboarding processes, and the answers caught me off guard. When I posed the question, "When you get to the point of deciding whether to accept a prospect as a new client, how do you decide?" I got answers totally unrelated to the description of the target markets. I heard adjectives such as *feel, fit,* and *comfort* or personality descriptors such as "delegator," "they buy into our process," "they followed up on advice," and "they did not raise strong objections to our fees."

In short, the decision about whether or not to work with the new client related entirely to the quality of the relationship and had little or no relationship with what advisors told me they were targeting.

An assessment of the quality of a client relationship can be an important element in interviewing prospects. But assessing whether a prospect fits your description of most desired client is also a critical element.

This raises a number of questions. Were advisors really embracing client segmentation? Were they oriented to attracting "A" clients, or was it just an exercise they went through as part of developing an annual marketing plan? (As in "OK, segmented clients into 'A' 'B' and 'C'—check that off the list!") Are some of those relationship parameters actually part of what defines an "A" client? How do we redefine our target markets to include what we are really looking for in prospective clients?

BE SPECIFIC ABOUT YOUR NICHE

It is my experience that when advisors address the idea of developing a niche or describing a target prospect, they are far too superficial in their approach. They write down some of the most obvious (and far too general) adjectives for their ideal client and stop before they drill down into those descriptions. If certain personality characteristics are shared by most of your best clients, they should be included in the description of your target. But before we start discussing a more sophisticated way of defining your ideal client, we should address the issue of whether advisors are actually researching their client bases even superficially. According to a recent study by Cerulli Associates, most financial advisors do not embrace formal segmentation.[4]

One of the fundamentals of referral marketing is being able to describe something unique that you can deliver to a specific kind of client. As in any field, specialists earn more than generalists. They also get referred more frequently. So it's surprising how few advisors embrace the concept. The Cerulli study found that only 37 percent of all advisors had a formal client segmentation plan, and only 26 percent of Registered Investment Advisors (RIAs) had one.

Many advisors believe that they have an intuitive feel for how their client base is composed and consider what they have is an informal segmentation plan. However, as the Cerulli study points out, "Though the informal segmenters are likely to believe that their process pays dividends with less commitment, their lack of dedication actually results in lack of implementation." I equate an advisor in this situation with a client who is satisfied with her undocumented, intuitive financial plan. Do you believe that you have done this kind of analysis on your client base? The test is whether you changed anything about your service mix or communication plan once your segmentation was complete. If not, you missed something.

When segmenting clients—or its cousin, choosing a target market—the biggest mistake I see is being too general. Remember, for people to refer you consistently, you must represent a clear solution for a type of problem or type of client. This is not possible if you have defined your ideal clients as "women" or "retirees" or, God help me, "individuals with at least a million dollars in investable assets." Your segmentation or targeting must address some characteristic or challenge that a (probably small) portion of the population shares and can relate to.

Highly compensated executives with substantial wealth in stock options, families who want their investment plans to reflect their Christian values, or couples with children from earlier marriages all represent groups with a clear need. The difference between the prior general segments and detailed descriptions such as these is the difference between heading "west" and heading to Fiji. They may start the same way, but the latter statement tells you vastly more about what it will take to get to the destination. It's a difference you need people to remember if you want them to mention you when the right opportunity arises. If you meet a father at a cocktail party and tell him that you work with "families," that's probably about where the conversation will end. But if that father has kids from a prior marriage and kids in his current one, and you tell him that you specialize in "working with the multiple-married, helping people protect the interests of the kids from their first marriage while providing for the kids of their current one," there is a better chance that you will have a conversation about it. And when your clients meet someone who is just about to get remarried to a wonderful woman with kids of her own, there is a much better chance they will mention you.

Target marketing or having a niche is widely written about in our field. But I know from personal experience and in my work with advisors that it is rarely seriously embraced. Part of the reason may be that the idea behind it is fundamentally against the DNA of most advisors. It is a problem born of our legacy. When you were new in the business, who did you accept as a client?

If you're like many advisors, you applied the "mirror test" to prospects. If they could fog one and had money in their pocket, they could become a client. You would basically do business with anyone who would do business with you. There was not necessarily a rhyme or reason to the people you brought into your practice. And so most advisors end up with what I call "the accidental practice." But that's not you anymore. Now you're successful. And now that crazy mix of client profiles is a service and, even more, a marketing problem.

YOU DON'T HAVE TO APPEAL TO EVERYONE

What kind of driver does Chevrolet specialize in? It is the economy car driver, of course—the person who is looking for an inexpensive and reliable way to get to and from where he or she needs to go because Chevrolet builds the Spark. No, excuse me, it is the environmentally conscious driver, for whom Chevrolet builds the Volt. Oh, wait, I'm sorry, it's the person who needs a vehicle to haul around a lot of things because

Chevrolet builds the Silverado and the Suburban. Obviously, it is the sports-car driver because Chevrolet builds the iconic Corvette. I have absolutely no idea who Chevrolet builds cars for. And I have no idea what someone might say that would trigger me to respond, "Oh, you should get a Chevy. You are exactly the person Chevrolet builds cars for."

Who does BMW build cars for? Regardless of the vehicle, BMW caters to the driver who is looking for something specific. In fact, as I write this, BMW has a new ad campaign on television. It shows each type of car the company builds in sequence as the announcer says, "We don't build sports cars, we don't build hybrids, we don't build SUVs, we don't build luxury cars. We only build one thing. The ultimate driving machine."

Most car buyers do not specifically want what BMW has to offer, or they are not willing to pay for it. That's fine by BMW. The company only wants one small piece of the market. And it has designed its products specifically for that one piece.

By the way, if you had invested in BMW in 2008, your position as I write this four years later would be up about 55 percent. If you had invested in General Motors, which produces Chevrolet, you would have nothing because the government had to take the company over.

Who are the highest-paid doctors? The specialists. Who are the highest-paid lawyers? The specialists. The same is true in financial services. In the 2010 Moss Adams financial performance study, the top-performing firms had a narrow focus and a product and service mix that was tailored to a specific audience. In 2009, Quantuvis Consulting found that advisory firms in the top quartile of performance had 68 percent of their clients in their target client category.

If you want to market effectively, you must specialize. And that means focusing on a specific profile of client while ignoring other worthwhile and profitable prospects. Although it is utterly against the DNA of most advisors, if you want to be a success at attracting referrals, you must choose not to pursue good prospects. I am surprised by how many advisors I meet who cannot bring themselves to commit to a market because it means not attracting some profitable clients.

Here's a classic example: I was conducting one of my Secrets of Referral Marketing workshops, and the group was discussing how to develop a niche. We talked about how specialization and aiming at a small part of a market can bring more clients than that advisor can service successfully. Think about it—if you are the one advisor that 1 percent of the people in your geographic area really need, how many potential clients is that? Where I live, that's about 800 households. So it's okay to basically ignore 99 percent of the population. If you can be the advisor with the most compelling value proposition for that target market, what do you need to achieve your goals? Ten percent of that potential market? Twenty percent? That could be 80 to 160 clients, a healthy-sized practice. And that's without leaving town. I can drive an hour east or west and have another market almost as big.

Everyone agreed. If we design an irresistible message for the 1 percent, we can accomplish as much as we would ever want to. Nods all around. Is everyone okay with that idea? Yes, all the participants say it makes perfect sense. We will determine who we can specialize in and create plans that will successfully attract that target market, even if no other prospects (outside the niche) respond to the message.

An advisor raises his hand. "So, if I meet a prospect outside my target at a cocktail party, and he has a rollover of $1 million, and I tell him what I do and it doesn't interest him at all, it's okay?" Yes, it's okay.

Immediately another participant objects. "But we have to say something that would get him interested—he would be a great client!"

From the day we enter the profession, we are trained to pursue any prospect who could be profitable. Eventually, we end up with a diverse client base that can be a challenge to service and a value proposition that attempts to attract everyone and is compelling to practically no one. When we first try to market to a target audience, we find ourselves unable to resist the temptation to say, "And I do that, too. And that. . . ." Focusing on a single, targeted client profile is counterintuitive, but less is actually more. Yet, as much as we have discussed it, many, maybe most, advisors still cannot bring themselves to focus on a single, targeted client profile.

Now let me make one clarification in terms of the people I accept as clients. There is a difference between what you go out fishing for and what jumps into the boat on its own. You need to be crystal clear and specific about who you want to attract as clients. Other people who do not fit that profile but would make good clients will find you. In many cases, there is no harm in accepting them as clients. In fact, some of them may become wonderful, profitable clients. If you find yourself being contacted by many people who you do not believe fit your target profile, there is probably something wrong with your marketing communications. And there are risks in taking too many people outside your target. But this doesn't mean that you cannot accept one occasionally. You may not have set out to attract that particular client, and you should not suddenly change your description of what you do and for whom, but bringing one in every so often is fine. Over time, however, you will want to develop your service mix and skill set in a direction tailored to the needs of your target market. Bringing in too many people outside your target can confuse or complicate that process.

TAILORING YOUR SKILLS AND SERVICES

However, if we want people to talk about us, to refer us, we need to be known for something specific and to provide those services to a specific group of people. And that means leaving a majority of the population out of your marketing and prospecting plans.

Narrow and deep beats wide and shallow. Less is more. Get known for being the single go-to advisor for something specific, and you can eventually get to the point where many of those prospects find you.

What you must do is answer a question: What is it that you have to offer and to whom? What particular solutions do you stand for? What particular experience will you deliver? When developing your target, you need to be able to deliver a solution for a group that is big enough to support a business but specific enough that people who are in that group will self-identify. That's the greatest concern I have about a target that is too broad. When I work with advisors, one of the biggest shortcomings in the way most advisors describe their target market is that it is far too broad. It is much too general for people in that group to identify themselves as part of it and too broad for people in that group to have a consistent financial need or challenge.

It is a rare advisor who can think past the clichés. Too many of us get hung up on the obvious answers: profession, demographics, club membership, religious community, social situation.

Now, obvious can be great. If you have specialized knowledge and a good network in one of these obvious markets, you can have a powerful marketing program. The big problem with the obvious answers, of course, is that there aren't enough of them to go around. If your target market is "doctors," you have an army of advisors competing directly with you and will have a difficult time differentiating yourself from most of them. Besides, most doctors don't think of themselves as "doctors." They think of themselves as pediatricians, rheumatologists, oncologists, and surgeons. In fact, it is pretty common to hear one specialist sniping about a doctor of a different specialty. Think of it in our own industry. All I have to do is get a broker together with a fee-only planner and refer to them both as "financial people" to have a good argument. So the broad, general categories we put people into are not sufficient.

One thing I have observed about successful advisors with loyal, dedicated clients, clients who provide referrals, is that many of those clients have something in common. It may not be profession, it may not be net worth, it may not be membership in some fraternal or social organization, but it's there. They have a good relationship with the advisor, and when they get together, they like each other as well.

WHO'S YOUR TRIBE?

Seth Godin, who has written brilliant work on marketing, refers to these groups as *tribes*. In a *Wired* magazine interview, he referred to a leader's or marketer's role in terms of creating and building a tribe. He described the process as "connecting like-minded people and taking them to a place they want to go."[5] I will add one more aspect for our discussion—taking that group to where they want to go the way they want to get there.

Your target market may not be easy to define in terms of profession, age, family status, or membership in a religious or fraternal organization. And that's okay. If you can define where a group of people wants to go, which in our profession should be easy, and the way they want to get there, you will have a good start on how to build your tribe. For many advisors, your tribe may be defined by your style of getting them there. The way you coach people toward their goals, the way you help them organize their financial lives, your particular approach to investment management may do more to define your target market than the clients' professions or net worth.

Godin points out that if you do enough for the tribe, it will grow. And what you can do for the tribe is to connect people with an issue and with each other. What defines your tribe? What are you doing to lead them? Clarify those nonobvious connections, and you may have a powerful idea to drive your marketing plan.

One advisor with whom I worked, Tim, started out by describing his target market as "women." Well, I'm sorry, but that's 52 percent of the population. It is impossible to come up with a particular need or set of circumstances that adequately describes or is shared by everyone in that target group. There is nothing meaningful that you can say that would tie together the financial needs of my 17-year-old daughter, a 45-year-old female corporate executive, and an 85-year-old widow. They are all women. But they belong to different tribes. I promise you that if you went to a cocktail party and someone asked you what you did and you replied, "I'm a financial advisor who works with women," you would elicit approximately no enthusiasm—even if you were talking to a woman.

It has to be more closely specified than that. It needs to be brought down to a level of detail where you can describe your target market and what needs its members have, and anyone in that target will instantly associate your description with their own situation. If they don't, you need to refine it further.

As I worked with Tim, I helped him to narrow his description. As it turns out, he actually worked with a fairly specific group of women, women who were taking charge of the family finances after their husbands had taken care of it for most of their adult lives. You see, Tim works in a city in the Southwest that has massive retirement communities. So the situation of a man passing away or becoming incompetent from Alzheimer's disease affects a meaningful proportion of the female population. And the women in those households have shared needs, shared anxieties, and shared experiences. The kind of advice one of them needs is the same as the advice most of them need. And their needs are not all financial. There are legal, psychological, and social needs they all have as well. That can be key because many of the financial services we provide are pretty much the same across different client segments. Whatever Tim is not qualified to provide, he finds resources to refer. Once Tim learned to describe his target market this specifically, his message became vastly more powerful.

Let me get up on my soapbox and rail against one of the most egregious mistakes an advisor can make in target marketing—that is, defining a target by income, net worth, or investable assets. People with more than a million dollars to invest are *not* a target market! Yet, in the "2010 FA Insight Study of Advisory Firms: Growth by Design,"[6] 70 percent of advisory firms reporting indicated that they use investable assets to define their target. As the authors point out in the study, "While life stage and level of assets may be a helpful starting point, they do little to assist a firm in successfully mining the market to find and attract new clients."[7] As Kitces observes about this finding, "In fact, as far as I know, most advisors include assets as part of their target client for one simple reason: They want to be certain that the client can afford to pay them." As the title of that blog post explains, people who can afford your services are *not* a target market![8]

Here's the thing—a target market works only when it constitutes a tribe. That is, when the people in it share common needs and challenges and—this is crucial—*they are looking for something in common and identify themselves with other people looking for that same thing.* To my knowledge, there is no bond like this among people based solely on their bank balance. I am a husband, a father, a stepfather, a small-business owner, a cook, a dancer, and an aspiring woodworker. If you tell me that you specialize in the needs of one of those categories, you might get my ear. If you tell me that you specialize in the needs of people who have the same amount of money in the bank as I do, you are saying nothing of interest to me. There are challenges I face that I share with other fathers and other small-business owners. There are no challenges I can conceive of that meaningfully tie together people who have $1 million of investable assets. So can we all just agree to stop saying, "I specialize in working with investors who have more than $1 million to invest"?

Mark Colgan is one of the best advisors I have ever met in terms of understanding how to market to a target. Mark was widowed as a young man and went on to specialize in the needs of survivors who had experienced a recent loss. He has gone on to work with clients who have enough to provide for themselves and now want to leave a legacy. The ages and professions of his clients are all over the map, but they share a common set of needs about which they feel strongly.

There are many advisors who work with small-business owners. As a group, owners of all small businesses have some things in common. They also have many differences. One advisor I worked with who had mastered his target market was Phil. Phil did not specialize in small-business owners; he specialized in the owners of machine shops.

If you have any small-business owners in your client base, you know that one of the requirements of a first appointment with them is to go on a tour of the business. Thus, when Phil met a new prospect, it was common for him to go for a walk around the shop floor at the end of the first meeting. They would not get too far into the tour before Phil said something to the effect of, "Is that a new Kellenberger cylindrical grinder?" (I am making this up—Phil is the expert on the machines, not me.) "Does that thing *rock*? I have heard it takes 25 percent off the time needed to turn a product. How has it been working out?"

As he walked through the plant, he would comment on specific machines and ask about specific challenges, such as quality of received materials and lubricating oil. What do you suppose the owner was thinking when Phil finally turned in his safety glasses and left? "This guy understands what I'm up against. He knows me. He is one of *us*."

Did any of that knowledge affect what kind of recommendations Phil gave to the business owner about his succession plan? Probably not. But the way the client felt about Phil was very different from the way he felt about the other "suits" who walked through the door.

But maybe it did affect the advice Phil gave. Dry cleaners, McDonald's franchisees, auto dealers, and other types of businesses have peculiar challenges all their own. If you are the person who speaks to them about their unique challenges, you will stand out from other people who want to provide them with financial advice. For additional help in developing your target market, you can download free worksheets at my website www.theclientdrivenpractice.com/worksheets.

When you start to narrow your focus, you will be describing your ideal client to give people a better idea of whom you want to work with, but you probably will not have a lot of specialized skills for that audience yet. You will be differentiating yourself from a marketing perspective. Once you begin to work with more people in that target audience, get to know in more detail their specialized needs and wants, and develop a learning plan around those unique circumstances, you will transform a marketing difference into a skill difference. At that point you actually represent capabilities that other advisors do not and that your target market finds especially valuable. And that leads to understanding and developing the next requirement of a referral marketing plan: a unique value proposition.

CHAPTER 4

WHAT'S SO SPECIAL ABOUT YOU?

Now that you know the kinds of people you're aiming to attract as clients, you must understand what is unique about you and why it makes you perfect for them. Critical to attracting clients and receiving referrals is a competitive advantage, a strategic differentiator, a unique value proposition—something that enables people to understand why they should choose you over all other financial advisors.

YOU MUST BE KNOWN FOR SOMETHING

When I work with advisors on understanding or developing their differentiator, I give them what I call the *cocktail party test*. Here it is: Imagine that you meet someone at a cocktail party, and the conversation winds around to what you do.

"So you're a financial advisor, huh? I'm glad I bumped into you. I've been looking for a new one and have met with three or four. So tell me: Why should I work with you and not with any of them?"

When I work with financial advisors on building their practices, this is one of the hardest questions we face. It is also one of the most important. Yet maybe only 10 percent of the advisors I talk to have a compelling answer.

In order to attract a new client, you must offer a reason why that client should hire you above all the other advisors she has access to. So what do you tell people? What is it that separates you from anyone else the client may interview? Since most of your prospects probably already have an advisor, you must offer something materially different from what the advisor the client has now is offering, or it won't be worth the trouble of moving the relationship. Have you ever had the experience of presenting to a promising prospect, explaining how your services are superior to his current advisor's, and failing to get a signature on the transfer form?

I hear this frustration frequently. Recently, I was coaching an advisor who found himself in such a situation with a particularly wealthy prospect. "I showed him how my portfolio would be better balanced than his account is now. He can't understand their statements. I showed him that my portfolio is less expensive because I use stocks and his broker uses mutual funds. He doesn't even *know* his broker—the broker was assigned to him when someone else left. And he keeps putting me off. I just don't know what to do next!"

"What is it about what you do," I asked, "that makes you the perfect advisor for him—better than anyone else and better than his current advisor?" Silence. The advisor had explained all kinds of ways a portfolio with his firm would be superior to the client's current portfolio, but he had never assessed what the client really cared about and why the advisor's firm was a better fit. It could be that the client didn't care that the portfolio would be better diversified or cheaper. (Really. I'm serious. I have known clients who have enough money not to care about what they are paying for portfolio management. Besides, you know better than to compete on price, right?) So my conviction is that the advisor was spending time talking about what *he* thought should be important, but in reality, that was not of significance to the client.

"WOW" IS NOT ENOUGH

I have been told that to attract referrals and clients, I have to provide a "wow" experience. But that's just not enough on which to base a business development or referral marketing plan.

Last week, I was discussing with an advisor his strategy for using his client advisory board to generate referrals. During the conversation, he said, "We have to make sure that we deliver such a fantastic experience that the clients will tell everyone about us." This is a philosophy I have heard many times. As a business-development strategy, it has some serious shortcomings.

One issue, of course, is that there is no generally agreed-on definition of *wow*. Too often, when I've heard an advisor say this, he then went on to provide his own interpretation of *wow*, and that is one way to disappoint clients. What matters is that you exceed the *client's* expectations, not your expectations of what the client wants. And all clients are different. For that matter, how will *employees* understand what *wow* is? And how can they deliver it if they cannot clearly translate it into behavior?

I remember one time I established a new relationship with a bank. There was some form that I neglected to sign or something. The manager, in her pursuit of delivering the "Wow" experience, drove to my office to deliver it to me. My reaction was, "Why is there a bank manager in my lobby? The mail would have done just fine. I don't need to be interrupted right now." My assistant went out to see her. The manager had dedicated a meaningful portion of her day to drive to my office to personally deliver something, as testament no doubt to the bank's dedication to delivering an outstanding customer experience. And if it had any effect on my attitude toward the institution, it was mildly negative. She focused on *her* assumptions of a great experience and ignored *my* expectations.

The bigger issue of "Wow" is that too many people say it. And yes, most do not deliver it, but *you* do. I know. But how will prospects know this? If a prospect interviews five advisors, and they all say that they deliver an amazing client experience, how will that help the prospect to choose you?

If you dedicate yourself to consistently delivering "Wow," how will you operationalize that? If you are committed to providing "Wow," you must have procedures around it, and they must be measured. It is much, much better to define exactly what your service comprises and explain that to clients. Better yet, ask potential clients if that is how *they* would define it.

A surprising number of clients are not particularly loyal to their advisors. I mentioned some survey results to this effect in Chapter 2. So it is not necessarily hard to get a client to show you her portfolio for a second opinion. But what do you bring back to the client once you have done your analysis? Is it that you identified a number of ways that you believe the portfolio could be improved? Or is it a discussion of why your firm is different in a way that better matches what the client really wants in an advisor? By giving you their current statements, clients actually may be making your job harder. By offering to do a portfolio analysis, you have now turned the conversation toward a discussion of why your investment-management process is better than what the client currently has. It is frequently the case that what makes your firm a better fit for the client does not actually have to do with investment management. And even if it does, I see too many advisors take the statements without asking the question you must ask if you are going to assess how you are a better fit: "If there was one thing you could change about how this portfolio is managed that would make you a happier client, what would it be?" By the way, if the answer is, "Nothing," you may be better off leaving the statements there—they will likely be a dead end.

IT'S PROBABLY NOT ABOUT THE INVESTMENTS

This statement probably will cause people to throw rocks at me, but I'm going to say it anyway: A lot of your clients may not actually care how you manage their portfolios. At a recent advisory board, one participant said, "I hate it when financial people go on and on about how they are going to manage my portfolio. I don't care! I just want to let them do it!" Another participant chimed in and added that what mattered to her was that the advisor would help guide him and coordinate the advice from all his advisors (i.e., accountants, lawyers, etc.). "If you can do a good job at that, you'll get my money. I assume that if you are competent, you will provide me with a market return. Just don't approach me and immediately ask for my money—that will turn me off right away."

Julie Littlechild discusses this in "Anatomy of the Referral."[1] She summarizes part of the report's research by saying that creating engaged clients is a matter of having the right clients, the right conversations, and the right questions. Part of the *right conversations* is working with the client on issues beyond the portfolio. Engaged clients are statistically much more likely to have some form of financial plan and to have it updated periodically. Differentiating yourself in most cases involves what you do for the client beyond managing the portfolio—especially if you call yourself a financial planner!

It turns out that even most financial planners don't actually do much planning, focusing instead on investment management. Industry research firm Cerulli Associates released a study in January 2012 that shows that while 59 percent of practitioners identify themselves as financial planners, only 30 percent actually offer financial planning services. While many offer some basic elements of financial planning, most offer what might more accurately be called *investment planning services*. One of the study's conclusions is that because of this widespread inconsistency in terminology, a "lack of clarity about what services an advisor actually offers investors is likely to continue."[2] Of course, what is a problem for the industry is an opportunity for you. Show clients what kinds of planning services you provide, and you can set yourself apart from a lot of other advisory firms.

YOU'RE PROBABLY WRONG ABOUT WHAT'S SPECIAL ABOUT YOU

What is it, then, that differentiates you? Most advisors I speak to do not actually know, although they believe they do. They make a fundamental mistake in understanding what a differentiator is. In fairness, this confusion is not confined to the financial services business. I find that it is true of business leaders in many industries.

In her book, *Creating Competitive Advantage*,[3] Jaynie L. Smith lists the 10 most common things CEOs say as to what makes them different. They are

- Good customer service
- Quality
- Reputation
- Good results
- Our employees
- Knowledgeable staff
- Consistent management
- Responsiveness
- Innovativeness
- Trust

I have participated in one of Jaynie Smith's programs. I was there with 11 other CEOs when she asked each of us to write down what we believed was the most important thing that separated us from the competition. Most of us listed the same things—the things on her list. When we went around the table reading our lists aloud, it took us until the fourth participant to finally get the idea. After all of us had spoken, Ms. Smith flipped the page on her flip chart, and there was almost everything we had listed, already written. It was a powerful point. If most companies say it, it is not unique.

Here is one simple exercise to help determine whether there is something about your practice that separates you from the competition: List the top three reasons clients should choose you over other advisors. Go ahead, take out a piece of paper and write down your reasons. Come back when you're done.

So what did you write? Are they three things that other advisors would not write or that other advisors could not claim? Probably not, and don't take offense. In their book, *Marketing for Financial Advisors*,[4] Eric T. Bradlow, Keith E. Niedermeier, and Patti Williams discuss responses to a survey in which advisors describe their value: "I have many years of experience," "Our practice is client-focused," "We deliver superior performance," and so on. Worthy attributes all. The issue, of course, is that nearly everyone claims them.

Thus, if everyone is telling prospects the same thing, how can they ever hope to tell you apart from your competition?

For most of our careers, we have been trained and encouraged to use the same clichéd terms. It is what we have been trained to say, and since we hear everyone else saying it, it must be right. Right? This part is hard. I have worked with hundreds of advisors and reviewed hundreds of advisor websites, and practically all of them say essentially the same thing. Many say *exactly* the same thing! I bet that I could copy the language off one advisor's website and paste it onto many others' pages, and the advisors who owned those sites would not even notice that I did it!

And let's get this out of the way right now—I know, everybody says it, but you actually do it. Got it. (If I only had a nickel for every time I have heard that. . . .) I know you are vastly better at whatever it is you say you're better at than the half-million other advisors in the country. Even so, here is the hard truth: When everyone else says the same thing, how is a prospective client to know that you really *are* better?

Even people who speak and consult in our field frequently get it wrong. At the Financial Planning Association's (FPA) conference Denver 2010, Vern Hayden, in his talk, "Differentiate or Die," gave a partial list of potential differentiators. But these, too, will not differentiate you:

- Fee-only
- Objectivity
- Being a Certified Financial Planner (CFP®)

These qualities are not differentiating. They are strengths, table stakes—what you have to offer just to be permitted to join the game. Can you imagine a financial advisor saying, "You should do business with us because it takes us a week to return a phone call, we have a terrible reputation, we provide mediocre results, and our employees are unresponsive?" Even if the things listed by Hayden could be differentiators, how would the clients ever know? Your service may be in a league by itself (assuming that you could prove it), but the fact is that everyone else says that, too, and a prospect cannot know it until after the purchasing decision. So how does it help to attract clients?

Let me take on one topic that has been (wrongly) emphasized in trade journals in the last couple of years. If advisors want to be more successful at attracting new clients, they have to get over their love affair with the fiduciary standard as a marketing advantage. It will not catch on. I have had my fill of breathless articles about how advisors are missing the boat by not marketing their fiduciary role. It ain't happening. Know why? Because it doesn't work.

For a differentiator to work, it has to be perceived as different by the prospect, and the prospect has to understand the idea. And fiduciary fails on both counts. The whole fiduciary argument is a relatively complex legal concept, and most clients don't understand it. It will not work as a marketing proposition for the same reason that mutual funds do not make headlines of their Sharpe ratios.

Clients are more interested in what you do for them and the service you provide than in how you get paid or what legal standard of care you must provide. What clients want to know is, "Will you look out for me? Will you put my interests first?" What broker would answer "No" to those questions? And when it comes to clients with existing relationships, the public's attitude in this arena is similar to their opinion about health care—the system is lousy, but I love my doctor.

Besides, if we are successful at persuading the regulators to make the fiduciary standard uniform across our industry, it will, by definition, cease to be a differentiator.

Another survey conducted by Cerulli Associates[5] revealed that almost twice as many clients prefer paying commissions to fees. About half of the 7,800 households surveyed preferred paying commissions, 27 percent preferred a fee based on assets, about 18 percent said they preferred retainer fees, and 8 percent opted for an hourly fee structure. (Hey, you NAPFA people, think about that for a few minutes. Half the people say they *prefer* paying commissions. Is that an informed perspective? I doubt it. But after so much talk about the superiority of fees, it says something about how much clients actually care about the method of compensation as a reason to choose an advisor.) About 33 percent of the investors surveyed said that they didn't know how they pay for the investment advice they receive.

The study also revealed that 63 percent of clients of the largest broker-dealers surveyed said that they believed their financial advisors were held to a fiduciary standard of care. This confusion appeared in another recent survey as well. In a J.D. Power and Associates survey released in June 2011,[6] 85 percent of the 4,200 clients of full-service brokers surveyed said that they had never heard of or didn't understand the difference between the suitability and fiduciary standards.

While they did not understand the regulatory issue that we all have been debating for the last few years, they had a very clear idea of what they wanted from their advisors—service.

"While higher levels of satisfaction are generally associated with clients in fiduciary relationships, . . . placing more focus on key best practices in client management . . . achieves satisfaction levels on par with satisfaction among investors in a fiduciary relationship," said David Lo,[7] director of investment services at J.D. Power and Associates. According to Lo, key best practices of client service include (in order of importance):

- Clearly communicating reasons for investment performance
- Clearly explaining how fees are charged
- Proactive advisor contact regarding new products and services or accounts four times in the past 12 months
- Returning client calls/inquiries within the same business day

- Reviewing or developing a strategic plan within the past 12 months
- Providing a written financial plan
- Discussing risk-tolerance changes and incorporating them into the plan where appropriate in the past 12 months

Do I support the fiduciary standard in providing financial advice? I do. From a marketing standpoint, however, it is a dead end. When I work with advisors to customize their practices for their target clients and create a marketing strategy around that, the most common struggle I have is getting those advisors to listen to their clients' ideas and opinions rather than pursuing their own. I believe that it's important that everyone operate on a fiduciary standard, but clients think we already do. If you want to stand out from your competition and win clients, find out from them what they believe is most valuable in an advisory relationship, and focus on delivering it to them.

THE COURAGE TO STAND APART

Why is it so difficult for advisors to develop a unique value proposition? Well, for starters, creative is hard. People who have learned to be creative make a good living because it is difficult to do. We tend to think alike. Thinking differently takes some skill. Second, it is not obvious. When I asked advisors what's special about them, or when I ask their clients that at an advisory board meeting, the first one, five, or dozen answers I get are the obvious ones. That's what occurs to us first. It is easy and tempting to take those first answers and try to move on to the next question.

Creative also takes courage. Marketing guru Seth Godin noted on his blog that setting yourself apart takes guts.[8] Like others before him, he points out that working harder is not going to make you more successful anywhere near as much as working smarter or differently. He also made a point I had not considered before—that simply getting more efficient at your work turns intellectual work into factory work. And that engages you in a race to the bottom.

Godin also noted that overcoming the inertia to get better at your craft or to be different in your profession and to create a competitive advantage requires taking a risk, and that takes guts. It is tempting to believe that everyone has chosen to do something one way because it's the best way. It is not—it is the average way. And it takes a measure of courage and self-assurance to make a choice that's different from that of your peers.

Ideally, a differentiator makes you unique. Separate. Apart. Think about how much easier it would be to get new clients and referrals if your clients could say, "Oh, you need to talk to my advisor—he's exactly the guy who does *that*."

Here is someone who might help: Scott Ginsberg, "that guy with the name tag," speaker, consultant, and author of *How To Be That Guy*[9] and other books. There is a lot I like about Ginsberg's approach, and about this book in particular, including the fact that one of the first quotes in the book is from Peter Montoya, another marketing consultant to financial advisors who has lots of good ideas.

One of the most useful examples in the book is right at the beginning. Ginsberg lists 22 questions for you to fill in, including, "After people get to know me, they'll never think about _____ the same way again," and, "There is

nobody walking the planet who could share the message about
_____ better than me."

Some of the questions highlight the challenges of marketing advisory services, such as, "If you Google the word
_____, the first 10 pages would be my website."
Try completing this question, and you will quickly realize why
telling people you "manage investments" will get your marketing plan exactly nowhere.

To attract clients and referrals, you need to be "that guy"
about something. George Kinder was "that life-planning guy"
and carried it to a national reputation. Roger Gibson did the
same as "that asset-allocation guy." Mark Colgan is headed
that way as "that legacy-planning guy."

WHAT GUY (OR GAL)
WILL YOU BE?

Do you specialize in succession planning for businesses? Do
you deal with multiple generations of the same family? I know
advisors who specialize in the needs of the "suddenly single"—
widows and divorcées. Lots of advisors do estate planning. At
Colgan Capital, Mark Colgan is a legacy planner, which creates a whole new dimension on top of estate planning.

Another principle of having a value proposition is to describe
your value in terms of the benefit a client realizes from working
with you. People care less about what you do and more about
what they get.

When I ask advisors what they do or what value they
represent, too many describe the process they use and not

enough describe the solution they deliver. People won't refer you because you have a customized financial planning process and evaluate individual goals and generate recommendations tailored to client-specific needs, and they won't refer you because you carefully monitor relationships between markets and rebalance portfolios based on proprietary protocols. Again, people care less about what you do and more about what they get.

WHAT SOLUTION ARE YOU?

I believe that the most powerful descriptions of the value that advisors offer encapsulate the benefits clients receive by working with them. The benefit must be something that your target market values. Consider describing what you do worded as a solution from the client's point of view. Complete this sentence: "People like [describe target prospect] come to me for [solutions that target market requires]. Here are some possibilities:

Corporate executives facing retirement in the next three years come to me because I show them the right choice on their retirement plan distributions.

Single professional mothers come to me to learn how to balance the demands of raising kids with the ability to afford college.

People who have saved enough to take care of themselves and want to use their savings to leave a mark on the world come to me to plan their legacy.

Don't worry about answering the question "What do you do?" with a sentence that starts out by describing your target client. You may think the person who asked you the question wants you to be the subject of the sentence, but you can get his or her attention much more effectively by starting with a description of the person you specialize in—especially if it is the person asking the question.

When I ask advisors what they do, most often I hear versions of, "I help people reach their financial goals" or "I manage people's portfolios to help reduce risk" or "I give people peace of mind." These are usually too general to be useful. And the bigger problem is that I don't think of my problems in those terms. I don't go to a financial advisor (or anybody but my therapist) looking for "peace of mind." I go looking for a solution or an outcome. I have just started a new business with one child in college, am newly married, working on consolidating two households, and have a three-year-old in the house for the first time in 14 years. You are *not* going to give me peace of mind. You might, however, be able to help me through the decision about how to save most effectively for college or work out the estate issues I face now that I have kids from two marriages.

People will come to get a solution, not to get a process. And people will remember to refer you because a friend mentions a problem that your client can plug your solution into, not because they like your process or because you have provided them with returns to keep up with the market (even if it's with lower volatility).

If you stand for process, you are a technician. If you represent a solution, you will attract clients and referrals who need a problem solved.

DELIVER A SOLUTION
OR AN EXPERIENCE

Ultimately, there are really only two things that we can deliver to clients—a solution or an experience. I believe that delivering a solution makes it easier to create a marketing strategy and to attract new clients. However, I have met enough successful advisors who cannot articulate a specific solution they deliver to clients that I have come to believe that clients also can be attracted simply to the experience an advisor provides. Examples of solutions might include optimizing college financial aid, understanding the planning effects of employee stock options, and minimizing taxes on large estates. Experiences might include making complex financial concepts understandable, providing reassurance in turbulent markets, being pleasantly persistent in getting clients to complete the steps they need to take in the financial plan, and doing things that make the client feel taken care of.

If it is an experience that you deliver, the description of your target market is likely to be less about specific life circumstances and more about psychographics. "Clients who are delegators" is an overused and oversimplified example. If you work with delegators, you will need to describe what kinds of things they look to delegate and how you carry them out for the term to be effective in your marketing.

Experiences as deliverables are more complicated to describe and take more testing with clients to confirm. Advisors I have worked with who deliver a certain kind of experience typically cannot define what the experience is when we begin to work together. "It's just how I do it" is where we start, and gradually we learn how that the approach is different from how other advisors do it and why it is attractive to clients. Advisors then can incorporate that description into how they communicate their value proposition.

Sometimes the experience is part advisory relationship and part social club or support group. The advisor I mentioned in Chapter 3 who works with women who have lost a husband or whose husband is incompetent is one example. This is a group that has consistent and significant social needs, and the advisor helps to facilitate connections with other similar clients. Another advisor I work with specializes in older single women and organizes potluck dinners and movie nights.

Tim Minert, director of concierge service for Redtail Technologies and a successful advisor in his own right, described to me in a phone interview how some advisors succeed because of their caring personalities. "They do things for clients, reach out on appropriate occasions, and send things to clients because they care," reports Minert. "They do these things naturally because it's who they are and not because it's a business-building strategy. But it ends up attracting them referrals." If this describes your practice, we just have to figure out how to describe it appropriately so that prospects can understand what the experience will be like and why it is different from the experiences they are likely to have with other advisors.

Sometimes what makes you different is specialized knowledge. Advisors of celebrities and international executives understand *kidnapping insurance*. Advisors of athletes have a particular expertise in *disability insurance*. Advisors of some medical specialties need to know how estate planning can work in conjunction with *malpractice coverage* or understand *asset-protection strategies* because of the risk of lawsuits. But the technical knowledge does not necessarily have to be that special.

STRENGTHS AS DIFFERENTIATORS

If specialized knowledge does not set you apart, your strengths can create competitive advantage. Jaynie Smith points out a short list of criteria: "It is objective, not subjective. It is quantifiable, not arbitrary. It isn't claimed by the competition. It is not a cliché."[10]

If you want to use a strength to differentiate your practice, measure it, document the process, make it a management priority, and hold employees accountable to it.

Just saying "Great customer service" won't do it. What truly makes it great? "We meet with our clients every quarter. All phone calls are returned within four hours. Our management team meets monthly to review our client contacts and outcomes. Here, let me show you our fully documented client-service process." Whatever it is must be written and measurable. Have your receptionist note in your client relationship management system when a client called. Create a report in that system to measure the time between when the call came in and when the call was returned. Review the statistics at management meetings. Include those reports in your employee performance evaluations.

Several firms I have worked with use their financial planning process as a differentiator. Saying that you provide financial planning will not set you apart from most other firms. These firms, however, had comprehensive, written processes for creating financial plans. One of them, especially, sets itself apart by giving a sample plan to every prospective client. They also encourage prospects to ask to see plans or get a sample plan from the other advisors they interview. Most prospects come back to report that all the other advisors they spoke with indicated that they also provided financial planning, but when the prospects asked to see a sample, they got a blank stare in return.

While identifying a differentiator is important, living it is critical. When the advantage you claim is not what the client perceives, there is something Jaynie Smith calls a "dangerous disparity." And, she says, "The most lethal form of dangerous disparity is to claim a competitive advantage and then fail to deliver it."[11] Once you decide on a differentiator, compare it with your client processes, discuss it with your staff, and measure your performance. Failing to live up to what you claim is your advantage is worse than not having a differentiator at all.

Living a strategic differentiator, on the other hand, will revolutionize your business. The ability to say and then prove that you deliver something people value, something that none of your competitors can do as well as you, gives you the opportunity to prevail in any market.

And if you don't have a differentiator? Create one. Choose a particular solution or aspect of the experience you deliver, and test it with your clients to see if it is what they consider the most valuable aspect of what you do. If you get a positive response, start focusing on that in your communications. As you get additional feedback about that proposition, make small changes in how you provide the service to focus on it and enhance it. The more you refine it, the better you can use it to set yourself apart from other advisors. You can get free exercises and templates to help you define and develop your differentiators at www.theclientdrivenpractice.com/worksheets.

Far more common than not having a differentiator is not knowing exactly what it is or how to describe it. Many of the advisors I have worked with began our relationship by saying, "There is nothing that ties all our clients together. They are all over the map. We just listen to them, take care of their needs, and manage their investments." But once we begin digging into who the clients are exactly and what specifically the advisor does for them, we frequently discover similarities among clients and specific things the advisor does that the clients value in particular. And that leads us to our next topic.

You may not know what it is exactly that sets you apart from other advisors, or you may think you know, but there is a group that knows far better than you do—your clients. Before we build a marketing plan around your target market and value proposition, we need to involve the people it affects and whom you want to attract. We need to get systematic client feedback.

CHAPTER 5

YOUR CLIENTS KNOW BETTER THAN YOU DO

In the last two chapters I asked you to develop your target market and your value proposition. But before we start using these as the basis of our referral marketing plan, we have one other important step—testing them.

One of the primary problems I see in advisor marketing is that it all comes from the advisor's head. Most of the articles and presentations I have seen that discuss developing a niche, describing a target market, and developing a value proposition regularly end with something to the effect of, "Now go lock yourself in a windowless room, and come up with it." That's not how the professional marketers do it.

When a serious organization such as Procter & Gamble, for example, sets out to come up with a new soap, its marketing department brings together the sort of people the company wants to sell it to and asks them for their opinions. What is missing from our product line? Would you be interested in a detergent that was more ecologically friendly? That smelled different? That was specially formulated for your wardrobe? The marketing people take that feedback to the product-development people, and that's what they start working on. But we tend not to. We tend to come up with the answer ourselves. And part of the reason for that is who we have to be as advisors.

WHY ADVISORS DON'T SEEK FEEDBACK

In our world, the client is the one who takes the advice. When we get a call from a frantic client after the market has just dropped 5 or 6 percent and the client wants to convert everything to cash, we need to be able to persuade him to do the right thing according to his situation, which may not be to convert to cash but may be to stay the course. These ups and downs are cyclic. We know that the market will come back. We know that things go up and then they go down. The strategy we have is a good strategy—stick with it, and it will pay for you in the end.

We're in the business of telling other people what to do. We have to take "No" a lot and keep pressing forward. But there is a dark side to these personality traits. The things that have helped to make you successful will complicate your life when it comes to marketing. Because we believe that we know what's right, and because we're in the business of providing advice to others, there is less inclination to look for advice ourselves, to go to other people to find out the answers to the question of what we should be doing to be most valuable. In terms of building your business and finding your value, though, there is only so much you can learn in the echo chamber of your own head.

Most financial advisors, when pressed to come up with a target market or to describe what makes them different from other advisors, have difficulty doing it. And when they do come up with a description, it tends to be in the technical jargon on which we're all trained to rely. They use those nondifferentiators that we're so fond of using to describe how we are different.

SOMEONE KNOWS BETTER THAN YOU DO

If you're like many of us, you don't actually know what sets you apart from other financial advisors. But there are people who do know, and they're your clients. They know why they chose you over other financial advisors and why they stay with you. They know the most valuable things you bring to the relationship. They know what you do that has meaning for them. Systematic client feedback is a critical element in a referral marketing program.

Just as important as knowing what clients value and what they consider unique is how they describe it. Your value proposition needs to be compelling to the people in your target market. This means that it needs to be in their words. We in the business have kicked around terms for segmenting clients and describing value long enough that we have settled into a very small vocabulary with too many technical terms. If I took all the ways I have ever heard advisors describe what they do and for whom, I bet I could write more than 80 percent of them with less than a couple dozen nouns and adjectives. Using those same words makes it difficult to distinguish yourself from other advisors. More important, it may not be the language your clients use at all.

I once interviewed Marc S. Freedman, CFP®, president of Freedman Financial and author of *Oversold and Underserved—A Financial Planner's Guidebook to Effectively Serving the Mass Affluent*. Discussing the importance of getting client input, he said:

> *You know, we all look at our businesses and say to ourselves, "I think I know what I can do to improve myself, to improve the way I market myself or improve the way the business looks. . . . I know what I need to do better." And after a while, we fool ourselves into believing that what we think we need to do is what we really need to do and we neglect to ask the people who are actually being impacted by the decisions that we make.*[1]

THE VALUE OF ASKING YOUR CLIENTS

Referring back to *Anatomy of the Referral*,[2] Julie Littlechild noted that asking the right questions was one of the three primary drivers of client engagement. Asking for and acting on client feedback were components of the relationships for a majority of engaged clients.

- Seventy-four percent of engaged clients said that they had been asked for feedback, whereas only 45 percent of the others said that this was the case.
- Sixty-one percent of engaged clients indicated that they felt that being asked for their input was very important or critical.

- Seventy-two percent of engaged clients said that the feedback they provided made a real difference.

The message? If you want engaged clients who consistently refer qualified friends and associates, make sure that you have an ongoing program of soliciting feedback, and improve your system and client expectations based on what you learn from that feedback.

More fundamental than learning to describe how you are different and your unique value in the clients' words, you may find that there is some significant work to be done to make you more referable.

The Institute for Private Investors (IPI) released a 2011 study that discloses some shocking statistics. If you are concerned about attracting and retaining clients, the study is something you must reflect on. Although AdvisorOne somehow translated the results into the headline, "Wealthy Investors Say They're Happier with Their Advisors,"[3] reading the study, entitled, "Both Sides Now,"[4] set off alarm bells for me.

The lead statistic is that 63 percent of ultrahigh-net-worth investors are fully satisfied with their advisor relationship. I don't know what your high school experience was like, but anything below 65 was a failure when I was there.

Shockingly, 95 percent of advisors said that their clients are fully satisfied. So 32 percent of advisors think that their clients are happier than they really are. Is it any wonder we are disappointed with the number of referrals we get?

Reinforcing that overall statistic, the study found, among other things, that 63 percent of investors agreed with the statement, "My advisor produces results in concert with my family's goals and risk parameters," whereas 17 percent disapproved of their advisor's performance.

A study released by investment management firm SEI in May 2011 about the importance of advisor objectivity[5] highlighted the emphasis clients place on their advisors' understanding their situation and needs. Failing to accurately understand client preferences and expectations will lead pretty directly to losing the relationship. Furthermore, a significant number of the investors in the study did not believe their advisors were using their full resources to the clients' benefit or providing adequate access. If you are the advisor to one of those clients, your relationship is at risk.

Fortunately, the IPI study also identifies the direction to a solution: "We are seeing a clear trend toward engaging in more of a partnership with the advisor, a natural evolution as investors learn more about due diligence in the aftermath of the financial crisis," reported Charlotte Beyer, IPI founder and CEO. "Advisors have longer-lasting relationships with investors who wish to be a partner in a dialogue." This reinforces Julie Littlechild's findings: When clients believe that their feedback is sought and implemented, they are more engaged, satisfied, and loyal. An ongoing dialog between an advisor and his or her clients is fundamental to driving client engagement.

THE CONVERSATION *IS* THE RELATIONSHIP

Poet David Whyte tells the story of a newlywed couple. The young bride wants to talk about their relationship. Although uncomfortable, the groom engages in the conversation, relieved when it is over. The bride, however, wants to talk more about it a few days later. The young man is frustrated when the following week she wants to discuss it again. He wonders, "Are we ever going to be done talking about this relationship, at least for a while?" Eventually, it occurs to him, says Whyte, "that this ongoing conversation he has been having with his wife is not about the relationship. The conversation *is* the relationship."[6]

The message is clear—involve your clients in an ongoing conversation, and discover how they really feel about your service. If you can uncover client disappointment about how well you leverage your resources for them, access to you, or the results you deliver, you have the information you need to give them the experience they desire.

As you work to increasingly thrill your clients, you will hear people tell you all kinds of things to do for them. But the key to driving client loyalty is not what gets told—it's what gets asked. I was rereading a post on Michael Kitces' blog[7] titled, "Nerd's Eye View," in which he points out that our value is not in what we tell our clients but in what we can motivate them to do. We too easily fall into the "expert syndrome." We believe that it is the quality of our advice that creates our value. While expert advice is a critical component of our service, without action, it does little good. I have seen this especially in fee-based planning practices. Since we are paid to dispense advice, it is easy to fall into the trap of stressing the telling rather than motivating clients to act. Unless clients act on our advice, we have not made their lives any better.

Acting makes for more satisfied, more engaged clients. Consider the difference between a client who describes her relationship with you to a friend as, "He gave me great advice," and one who tells her friend, "He got me to take these steps, and I'm way better off because of it."

Motivating to action is more about questions than answers. In his blog post, Michael Kitces describes a session at an FPA Retreat led by Karen Miller-Kovac, chief scientific officer of Weight Watchers. Ms. Miller-Kovac referred to *motivational interviewing* as a way to help clients discover the importance of change and to realize that they can accomplish it.

Similarly, my work with advisors continually reinforces the importance of questions over answers. Rather than telling prospective clients, "This is where our practice is headed, and these are the services we provide," it is far more powerful to ask, "What can we do that would be of the most value to you, and what would be the best way of doing it for you?" In my own client engagements, I always start a new relationship with the question, "What would have to happen in our working together that would cause you to believe it was a huge success?" Discovering what clients most want, from themselves and from you so that you can deliver it to them, is the most valuable service you can provide.

Have you ever lost a client? Do you know why? Shari Harley, president of Candid Culture, thinks you probably don't—so you might just be lucky you haven't lost more.

One of the better workshops I attended at the Financial Planning Association's (FPA) conference Denver 2010 was Harley's session on asking questions. One of her most important points was that clients don't tell us what they want—they just expect us to know. Unfortunately, as she joked, those clients don't come to our conferences. So you will have to incorporate it in your individual engagements. She also conducted an interesting exercise: List five prospects who left, and list the reasons why.

The most intriguing of the questions Harley asks her clients is about pet peeves. This is something that never occurred to me to ask. It offers the opportunity to avoid the worst-possible reason to lose a client—because you did something that was annoying without realizing it. An example she offered was a client whose pet peeve was being late. For almost all her meetings, she was consistently 15 minutes early. One time, however, she arrived 5 minutes late. A year later, the client was still referring to that particular meeting and her tardiness. It amazed Harley that it continued to come up in conversation, so she asked. It turns out that being kept waiting is that client's pet peeve. It didn't matter how many times Harley had been early—the one time she was a little behind schedule was the one that lived in the client's memory. Picky to the point of being silly? Sure. But that doesn't change how much it annoyed the client. And it is absurdly easy to avoid if you know about it ahead of time. Include in your onboarding process a few questions to ensure that your service is just what the client wants. And keep asking questions after the person has become a client.

The cornerstone of the client-driven practice process is soliciting client feedback. While I am mostly concerned with clients as a group, this is just as true on an individual basis. From client to client, in fact, you have an opportunity to tailor your service. Maybe not really to customize it, but to enable the client to select from a number of options you can easily (and probably do) offer. Would you prefer to meet or keep in touch by phone? Be contacted by phone or e-mail? In the morning or the evening?

You can turn it around as well. You know what a financial advisor does, but does your client? How thoroughly do you discuss expectations on both sides when you take on a new client?

For clients who are not new, you can begin by adding a few questions at the end of your meetings. You might ask, "Now that you have been with me for a while, what do you find most valuable about what I do for you? What is it that you appreciate most about the advice I provide?" However, to begin gathering systematic information on your clients' feelings and opinions, you will need to step up to another level of gathering client feedback. A good first step would be to conduct a client survey.

CLIENT SURVEYS

A survey can give you a 50,000-foot view of your practice. It enables you to get indications about how clients feel about the different aspects of your practice and to generate statistics on their opinions. These measurements can be compared with industry benchmarks, or they can be used as a baseline in evaluating how subsequent changes and improvements to your practice affect your clients' satisfaction. You can evaluate generally how well clients feel tended to and how prepared they feel for their future. You can propose new services and test for interest within your client base.

You can get this valuable feedback easily and inexpensively. While there are some Internet-based survey tools available and you could compose your own mail-based survey, asking the right questions and wording them the right way are a science. Julie Littlechild, author of the survey I have referred to many times in this book, is president of Advisor Impact, a company that specializes in performing client surveys for financial advisors. The company's surveys are written by experts and have been thoroughly tested with thousands of clients, and they are extremely reasonably priced. If you consider doing a client survey, I would strongly recommend speaking to Advisor Impact.

While survey data are very useful, they have their limitations. The feedback you will receive is based on static questions and most often a limited range of multiple-choice answers. For more detailed feedback, you will need to turn to a client advisory board.

CLIENT ADVISORY BOARDS

A client advisory board is a group of your best clients that would meet several times a year to discuss a limited agenda of questions dealing with the nature and quality of the services you provide. A very small number of advisory firms use an advisory board, but most of those who have done it well report that it is one of the most powerful business-development tools they have ever seen.

While the board invariably would include some of your biggest clients, the ideal group would consist of people you consider to be your "best" clients—the kinds of people who represent your target market and who you would most like to replicate. You want a blend of people who also represent your best clients as well as the best combination of personalities for the group dynamic. Just as in planning a shopping mall, the first thing you will want to identify is your "anchor" tenants. These should be clients who—because of the size of the relationship, their influence in the community, their influence in the target demographic, their dedication to the firm as expressed by the amount of referrals offered, or the quality of the input they are likely to contribute—would be vital to the success of the advisory board. You want to make sure that you have people who would be the answer to the question, "Who must be in the room to make this discussion a success?"

Some advisors believe that they need to invite their biggest clients. While some of your biggest clients will be represented on the board, limiting participation to that criterion will prevent you from getting the most value from the discussion. Some of your biggest clients may not represent the target prospect you wish to pursue. Many of us have some clients who regularly offer us valuable insights and advice, even if they are not particularly large clients. And if you are serious about involving your board strategically, involving it in significant business decisions for your practice, you may wish to gather participants with a particular professional expertise that may not be represented on your staff. If you bring marketing questions to the advisory board, for example, it could be useful to include a client who is a marketing professional. If you have staffing issues, a human resources professional from your client base would be a valuable participant.

It would be hard to exaggerate the benefits of conducting a live facilitated discussion about your practice with some of your best clients a few times a year. Firms who have consistently engaged in advisory board meetings report that their board members have become some of their best referral sources, even if they were not prolific referrers before. And when you get some of your best clients involved more deeply in your practice, how could you help but have a great outcome? John Gugle of Alpha Financial Advisors says, "The best referrals we have gotten on an ongoing basis have come directly from board members because they have a sense of empowerment, they have a sense of ownership in the firm, they have a real 'buy-in' in terms of what we're doing. They understand our message very clearly, and they can go out and articulate that more concisely to people they know."[8]

Brad Gardner, president of Emerson Investment Management, says of his firm's five-year experience with an advisory board, "We have learned a lot about what our clients are looking for and how we can enhance our services. We also believe that we are in a sea of sameness among investment advisors, and this would be a great way to differentiate ourselves to prospective clients."[9]

An advisory board enables you to explore questions in detail, exposing nuances and areas of gray that a survey cannot reveal. In answering survey questions, a client may think, "Well, it's not really A, and it's not really B, but it's closer to B than to A" and check off B. The advisory board setting allows you to explore why it isn't A and why it isn't B.

An advisory board can offer you more than feedback—it can provide guidance. And unlike individual client meetings, board meetings provide an opportunity for clients to hear each other and add to the thoughts and ideas of other clients. When they start inspiring ideas in each other, there is a magic that happens.

When you establish a client advisory board, the first couple of meetings must be all about the clients and their experience. This is the time to find out, in their words, why they chose you as their advisor and why they continue to work with you to the exclusion of other advisors. This is when you should ask them what's unique about you and what you do that they believe contributes the most value to your relationship. You can even ask who they believe you should be targeting as clients.

Most advisors convene their advisory boards between two and four times a year. I also recommend that they have a strategy for rotating clients onto and off the board. Board members generally serve two- or three-year terms, and the terms are staggered. Between one-third and one-half of the board retires each year, and new members take their places. This helps to maintain consistency on the board while providing for a regular infusion of new people with new ideas.

Once the board has been meeting for a year or so, you can begin turning attention from the client experience to the practice. Board members are more than just the voice of the clients. Used most effectively, they are advisors to your business as well. In my observation, one primary factor in the success of a client advisory board and the degree of impact that it has on the advisor's practice is whether the financial advisor uses the board strategically.

There are many issues and questions you can ask an advisory board to discuss. On one level, there is getting feedback. How do you like my new reports? Is there the right level of detail in my financial plans? Do my portfolio reviews cover issues in enough depth? Do I respond to your calls and questions quickly enough? This kind of information is useful and can help you to make some adjustments to improve your practice.

On another level, you can engage a client advisory board in determining how to address an issue that you believe clients may be concerned about. Specifically, they can be crucial in designing a communication strategy for a major event such as the retirement of a partner, a proposed merger, or changing broker-dealers. Getting guidance from some of your best clients on how to address these kinds of issues can mean the difference between success and failure of the transition.

Emerson Investment Management knows the value of getting client guidance in its marketing message. Among the issues it has brought to the board is its marketing communications. First, Emerson sought the board's guidance on determining its differentiator, its competitive advantage. One of the clear messages was that the clients appreciated the depth of the relationship the firm had with them, what managing director Stacy Austin Reinhart describes as "stickiness."

Thus the firm retained a marketing consultant who developed a campaign around the slogan, "Invested in Relationships." The folks at Emerson liked that and thought it reflected the clients' feedback well. Before proceeding, though, the company brought the new campaign to the client advisory board.

The board unanimously disliked it. They felt that it didn't connect with them, that it felt impersonal. But they worked on it. After some discussion, they made a small but significant change: "Invested in You."

Everyone on the board expressed the feeling that it spoke to them, that it was more personal, and that it accurately described their feelings about their experience with the firm.

As part of its thank-you, Emerson brought a special treat for the board members at their next meeting. "We bought everyone sticky buns," said Reinhart.[10]

Freedman Financial had a similar experience when testing an advertising campaign with its advisory board. The firm brought three versions of a video trailer to get the clients' impressions. Board member Sumner Feinstein describes their reaction: "Many of us weren't particularly impressed with that trailer. We told them where we thought it was not reaching us—there was no emotional grab there."[11] They made some changes and went on air with a version the clients believed connected much better with them.

DESCRIBING YOUR VALUE

Your best clients know how to describe your value better than you do. They live it; it's personal. And if you want to connect with more people like them, it will pay to seek their guidance when you develop your marketing messages.

The most valuable kind of engagement with your client advisory board is determining the strategic direction of your practice. What kind of client should I serve? Am I providing the right mix of services, or should I add or discontinue some? What should I do with clients who no longer fit my target market? Questions such as these can alter the fundamentals of your business plan. This is why they hold the potential to be the most valuable kinds of discussions you can have with your best clients.

They are also some of the scariest questions an advisor can put before an advisory board. What if the clients want the practice to go in a different direction than you want it to go? What if the clients recommend that you discontinue one of the services you consider to be most important or most valuable? What if the board urges you to pursue a strategy that you don't believe will work? What makes those issues so scary is what makes them so valuable. Is it more important to implement what *you* think is best or to run your business according to what your best clients want most? If your clients believe that you are willing to tailor your business to their wants and needs, and you communicate the changes you make through a newsletter, your website, or direct correspondence with your clients, their loyalty and level of engagement can increase dramatically. Do not fear their answers! Marc Freedman is a good example of how this fearlessness can pay off:

One of the toughest questions we ever asked our client advisory council was, "Why do you stay?" When the markets went down for months and years, every time they opened their statements, their investments were worth less, less, less. Did we have the guts to ask our clients, "Why do you stay? Why are you still here?" We did. And I think every advisor would be refreshed to hear the reasons why the clients stay.[12]

Engaged clients who are convinced that you will do anything within your power to satisfy their needs the way they want them served will reward you with more business and more referrals.

ZEN MIND

You will not always get what you want to hear from your advisory board. Scott Carlberg, a member of Alpha Financial's client advisory board, says, "John had some ideas on how the business should be run and what might be important to clients. In some cases we confirmed what he thought, and in other cases we said we understand what you mean and we don't like it. And he had to respond."[13]

If you want a greater share of wallet and more referrals, you need to periodically listen to and act on feedback. When it is time to receive that feedback, it is critical that you be in the "learning mode." When I facilitate client advisory boards, I coach advisors to have a "Zen mind." I encourage them to be in a state of openness. It's a little like practicing a form of meditation called *mindfulness*—accept ideas as they arrive, examine them without judgment, perhaps set them aside for further consideration, and move on to the next suggestion.

Getting into and staying in the learning mode are hard. As humans, we have a reflexive tendency to respond to questions with answers. Compounding that, we are in the business of providing answers. It is our job to share our expertise and tell people what to do. There are times, however, when we need to switch roles and get feedback on what we're doing. If we want to improve our practices, we need our clients' guidance. And in that situation, answering does not help. What do you learn when you answer? Nothing. How do you get better when you answer? You don't.

Always seek value in these interactions. Ask, "What can I learn from this client? What can I learn from this situation?" Look for questions to ask. If you are asked a question, try following the answer with another question. If possible, ask a question instead of answering. Here are some examples:

Before I answer that, what about this is important to you?

What would it mean to you if I could do that?

What would you say is the biggest concern you have that is prompting that question? (Which is a less threatening way of asking, "Why do you ask?")

The need to discuss this was highlighted by a conversation I had with an advisor just the other day. We were discussing the agenda for his first client advisory board meeting. He said, "I'm not sure what to put on the agenda. I don't know what they want to hear about." My response was that a meeting such as this was not about what they wanted to hear; it was about what they had to say.

There is a time to answer. When it is the time to listen and the client's turn to speak, the longer you can stay in the learning mode, the more your clients will tell you how to do more business with them and how you can attract more clients like them.

AN INDEPENDENT FACILITATOR IS KEY

One of the most important keys to success in having a client advisory board is to have a third-party facilitator. While I believe in the value of a professional, the most important thing is that it not be you. John Gugle has one of his clients facilitate his board meetings. To realize the most significant benefits of an advisory board, it's important that you be sitting with the clients as part of the group. They need to see you as an equal in the conversation—part of the tribe. This cannot happen if you are running the meeting from the front of the room.

A facilitator can serve as a sounding board or a target for criticism that clients would not be comfortable saying directly to you. People don't want to criticize you, especially when you're buying them a nice dinner. Criticism and expressions of concern uncover the value in the process. The conversation doesn't yield much until a client says, "I really don't like. . . ." Jackpot. You have uncovered an issue that, when addressed, can change the client experience for the better. Once clients see you involved in the conversation and see that you are willing to discuss things that may concern them, they know that they have permission to bring up any other issues they may wish you would fix or improve. But this requires that you be sitting at the table and that the clients see you as part of the group. And it requires that someone different be standing at the front of the room guiding the dialogue.

A facilitator also can help to prevent you from giving responses that shut down conversation. There is a natural human response to defend against criticism, however minor. But the right response is imperative. For example, I've heard clients say, "This other advisor provides these services much better than you do," and I've heard advisors respond with a version of "Let's review why we provide this service this way, and if you think we should change it, we can discuss it." Although subtle, the message here is, "You are wrong. We know how to do this," and it stifles the conversation. An experienced facilitator knows to respond more in the vein of "What do you like most about how that other advisor does it?" Pursuing such a conversation gives you vastly more useful information.

An independent facilitator can get away with asking some questions you, as the advisor, could never ask. Let's say a board member suggests a new service and other participants respond positively to the idea. Consider the question, "What do you think would be the best way of delivering a service like that?" From a facilitator, this appears to be information gathering. If the advisor asked the question, it might feel like a sales pitch.

FOLLOWING UP WITH THE BOARD

After each advisory board meeting, assess what you have learned, and follow up with the participants. When I conduct board meetings, each advisor gets a packet from me about a week later with a transcription of the recording of the meeting, a transcription of the flip charts of notes that we produced during the meeting, a summary of the discussion for the participants, and a summary and report for the advisor of what I believe we learned. Each person who was at the meeting receives a copy of the participants' summary. The report shows the board member the advisor's perspective on the issues discussed. More important, it demonstrates that the advisor is giving consideration to the advice he or she received. Which brings up the most important element of a client advisory board meeting—the commitment to act on the information communicated during the discussion.

It can be powerful to ask clients how you can improve their experience. It is far more powerful to demonstrate your orientation to client service by taking that advice and making changes. Conversely, receiving feedback and taking no action is worse than never having asked in the first place. Creating an advisory board implies a commitment to making changes.

For example, Emerson Investment Management was about to release a new website when the firm showed the design to its advisory board. The board expressed clear feelings about some basic changes. "The website was on the verge of going live, and we quickly went back to the designers. We're glad we did it," says Meghan DeTore, Emerson's director of marketing.[14]

When Freedman Financial floated the idea of an automated call routing system, the board's negative feedback was unequivocal. The firm's phone continues to be answered by a person.

Over the long term, a practice that systematically incorporates its board's suggestions will gradually be tailoring the client experience to its target market. Customizing your service mix, procedures, and environment to your best clients is a powerful driver of referrals.

During your first advisory board meeting or two, you will be testing the description of your target market and your value proposition. You will be checking with your clients to see whether your description of what ties them together rings true to them. You will be asking whether what you believe is the real value you deliver is what they perceive to be most important in their relationship with you. Be open to the possibility that they may have a different perspective on it. Your clients may attach significance to aspects of your relationship that you did not think to be particularly important. More likely, they may not have any strong feelings about something that you believe to be central to the service you provide. Listen to them. If they express little interest in the details of your investment management process, your best prospects likely will feel the same way. If they tell you that coordinating the advice between their accountant, their attorney, and you is tremendously valuable because of how it simplifies their lives, there is a good chance prospects will be strongly attracted to it, too.

For more information on putting together your advisory board, download my free white paper. You can find it at http://www.theclientdrivenpractice.com/advisory-board-white -paper/.

Now that we have tested them and have clarified what you do and for whom, we can begin the process of establishing your firm as the authority on it.

Update the description of your target market and your value proposition to incorporate your clients' feedback.

CHAPTER 6

OWNING A SPOT ON THE CLIENT'S BRAIN

So far we have created a detailed description of the kind of client you can best serve and have defined just what kind of value you can deliver. We have systematically collected feedback from clients and centers of influence to check to see whether that audience and that value rang true to them and whether they agreed with what you believe are the most valuable parts of what you do. Having confirmed and clarified what you can uniquely deliver to your target clients, you now must become the person who embodies that value to those clients.

Now that we know the unique value proposition you represent, your objective is to achieve what I call "owning that spot on your client's brain."

You know that referrals happen when one of your clients or centers of influence hears someone describe a problem that you would be particularly good at solving and then mentions you to that person. For most advisors, the most difficult aspect of leveraging this natural process is that they do not represent a specific kind of solution, or they do not clearly communicate that specific solution to clients. You must accurately describe the benefit you represent so that whoever hears it can recognize its value and recall it when a friend describes the issue it solves. Most clients do not have a clear idea of what specific scenario you are best qualified to help people with and so will not recognize the best times to mention you. When the opportunity arises, no referral will be made. Successful referral marketing is mostly about preparing clients for the opportunity to refer you.

Julie Littlechild's research[1] shows that as many as 93 percent of your clients are willing to refer you to others. I have heard plenty of clients say to advisors, "Tell me how I can help you get new clients." A large part of referral marketing is training clients and centers of influence to make a referral when the moment is right—teaching them how to help if they are willing.

BECOME THE BRAND

Owning a spot on your client's brain means that you have described and reinforced the specific kind of client and client problem in which you specialize so thoroughly that when anyone describes that problem to one of your clients, he cannot help but have you pop into his mind. Your goal is to establish so firmly in your client's mind the particular prospect circumstance you seek that when someone describes it to him and tickles that spot on his brain, your name naturally will fall out of his mouth.

Every time you describe what you do and for whom—on your website, in your marketing materials, and in the articles and white papers you write—you must reinforce that special skill and value. Everything about how you describe your practice needs to promote that particular benefit and advance your claim on that spot in your client's brain a little bit further.

When you can make your firm synonymous with the solution your target clients are looking for, new business will arrive automatically.

When you need to blow your nose, what do you call the thing you reach for? A Kleenex, of course. But that's not what it is. It's a facial tissue. So why don't we call it that? Because the brand Kleenex has done such a superior job of identifying itself with the solution a facial tissue represents that we all have come to call the generic solution by the brand name. We might ask for a tissue, but it is highly unlikely that we would ask for a Puffs or a Scottissue or a Windsoft. Even if we buy one of those brands, there is a good chance we still ask someone to pass us a Kleenex.

When you want canned fruit suspended in a jiggly green mold, what do you look for? Jell-O. And if you say Jell-O to anyone, they know instantly what you're talking about, even though it is not the only brand of instant gelatin. And although it is not quite as common as it used to be, the verb for duplicating documents used to be *Xerox*. As in, "Would you please Xerox this in time for the meeting?"

So what does all this have to do with financial advice, anyway? The idea of your brand becoming identified with a particular solution or experience can help you to build your firm the same way it helped those consumer products to achieve market dominance.

Rob Brown is an attorney who specializes in employee stock ownership plans. It is all he does. While his firm goes by the typical Four Names, LLP, its website is www.esopplus.com.

He has a national reputation for counseling business owners who are interested in the idea of employee ownership, and not just as a succession strategy. Perhaps most impressive, partners at large regional and national law firms unhesitatingly refer clients to him if the topic of employee ownership comes up. (Most of the time, partners in larger firms will refer only to specialists within their own firm. You can get some serious demerits for referring business outside the firm.)

I see lots of financial advisors who promote their expertise in working with business owners. And all of them also have expertise with lots of other types of clients—corporate executives, doctors, retirees. Okay, let's say it: They have expertise with everyone. Or at least so many kinds of clients that the recognition they can get for just one type is diminished to nothing. None of these advisors will accomplish what Rob Brown has. They will not be able to develop even a local reputation as the one advisor to go to if you are a small-business owner because they want to "specialize" in everyone. Therefore, they represent no one in particular.

You may not be able to become the Kleenex of financial advisors, but following Rob Brown's example, you can become the one person everyone thinks of as the solution to a particular problem. In a large portion of the financial and legal community in the Northeast, Rob Brown now "owns" the real estate on everyone's brain labeled *employee stock option plan*. And when a business-owner client mentions that term to her attorney or wealth advisor, there is a good chance Rob's phone will ring.

Developing a unique value proposition is really the hard part. But I am amazed at how even advisors who have a powerful and unique offering miss the opportunity to promote it in their marketing or when they talk with people. An advisor not long ago attended one of my seminars. In speaking with him after the event, I asked what was unique about his practice. He described his process for identifying and analyzing alternative investments for high-net-worth investors that truly separated him from most of the advisors with whom I speak. The way he described it was, "I do the research it takes to identify investment opportunities that 99 percent of financial advisors never hear about." So I gave him the cocktail-party test from Chapter 3. "Let's say I meet you at a cocktail party and ask, 'What do you do?'" His response? "I'm a financial advisor."

Is he kidding? He does something that, by his own account, clients might be able to get from 1 percent or less of financial advisors, and he doesn't mention it? Is he afraid people might be interested and, heaven forbid, want to hear more? Is he trying to *avoid* getting new clients?

I am surprised at how often this is the case for practitioners who do something special for their clients. It just honestly does not occur to them that when people ask you about what you do, they would be thrilled to get an interesting and provocative answer. Maybe some advisors believe that the tired, old generic answer is somehow what they are *supposed* to say. As I have mentioned before, I also know that some people are scared of giving an answer that would put them in a box and potentially turn off or fail to engage some of the people to whom they speak. Get over it. You want to catch the interest of only a small part of the population. But you want that small part to be dying to meet you. And that can only happen if you describe your value in a compelling way.

To own a spot on your client's brain requires that every one of those moments of truth, when you have the opportunity to expose someone new to the value you deliver, your core message reinforces who you are and the amazing thing you can do for your target client. You always must be communicating that you are not for everyone, but to the people whose needs you specialize in, you're the *only* one. The people with whom you talk may not be in that population. If that's the case, there's no harm in not attracting them. But they may know people in your target group. And if they do, you want them to be talking to those prospects about how perfect you sound for them. *That* is a referral.

YOUR ELEVATOR SPEECH

To stake out the cerebral real estate you want to claim, you will need a brief, concise, and compelling way of describing what you do—the response to the cocktail-party question. This is what most sales guides refer to as your *elevator speech*.

You probably have an elevator speech—a brief description of the benefits you deliver to clients that enables you to communicate the value of what you do simply. (Ideally, it's worded as a solution; see Chapter 4.) I'm going to suggest that you actually have two speeches, the first to get them to focus on you if they are prospective clients and the other to give them a reason to come talk to you.

To be effective, an elevator speech must first capture their attention and then communicate your value. If you have not successfully captured their attention, no message will get through. We all have thoughts running through our head all the time. Frequently, they have nothing to do with what we happen to be in a conversation about. We're thinking about the grocery list. Or the bad meeting we just left at work. Or the pretty girl across the room.

If we can break through those preoccupations, we can test for interest. If there is no interest, any message we deliver will be ineffective.

Here is the idea: Have a short, direct statement to grab attention and test for interest. Imagine that you say, "Freelancers come to me to help them assemble a benefits package like the one they had in the corporate world." And the person responds, "Interesting. Was that Red Sox meltdown the most amazing fail you ever saw?" If this happens, you know what you need to know—this new friend is not your target. And you have just spared both of you the time it would take to deliver a pointless and unnecessary description of your work.

However, if the person is in your target market, she might respond, "Really? I thought I would have to leave benefits behind when I started consulting. How do you do that?" You now have her attention, and she has qualified herself. You have permission to tell her more, perhaps another three or four sentences. You can list a few challenges that your clients face and describe the unique expertise you offer to overcome them.

Too many advisors have little idea how to communicate the value they deliver. Some have given it some thought and do a decent job describing what they do, but in a way I would find uncomfortably long if I had no interest. There is a reason it's called an *elevator speech*. The idea is that you should be able to deliver it to a prospect on an average elevator ride. The time limit I have usually heard is 11 seconds. But a lot of the answers I get to my cocktail-party question go on for a full paragraph. I like the idea of a short elevator speech being less than five seconds. I used to have a radio program—five seconds can be a long time. If the person you're talking to is interested, you have permission to go on a little longer for the second step.

SAMPLE ELEVATOR SPEECHES

I also have heard the suggestion that you should have different elevator speeches for different audiences. I must emphasize, however, that these different versions should not communicate different value propositions. Thus, for example, if you specialize in the needs of high-level corporate executives, do not have an elevator speech for physicians and for retirees. That is exactly the mistake I noted earlier—the opposite of having a focused practice. If you want to own a part of your client's brain, you need to know which specific part you want to own. However, that particular specialty may look or sound different to people looking at your target population from different angles. Thus you can have several versions of the same basic talk tailored for different audiences.

Therefore, for example, if you work with small-business owners on their retirement benefit plans, you would have one version of your elevator speech that emphasizes how you can improve the wealth of small-business owners to use when you meet an entrepreneur. When you find yourself talking to a certified public accountant (CPA) in a social situation, you might describe what you do for those business owners from a tax- or operating-plan perspective. When you meet a corporate attorney, you might describe what you do for business owners from a third perspective. Your target market and your unique value remain consistent, but you're describing them from three different angles.

I also should address one other variation of the elevator speech that seeks to be clever more than it seeks to communicate value. Jay, a friend of mine who has been a financial advisor for several decades, likes to respond to the cocktail-party question with, "I am a social worker for the rich." Invariably this provokes a response such as "Excuse me?" or "You're a what?" It succeeds in breaking people's attention and gives Jay the opportunity to continue: "Family stress is created more by money than by anything else. And the more you have, the more there is that can cause that stress. I take care of people's financial affairs so that they can focus on family and career without anxiety."

I cannot say that this is the wrong approach. Clearly, it works for Jay. It breaks people's attention, which is good. If whatever you say provokes a request for more information, you're on the right track. It frequently starts conversations. It is memorable. All these qualities help to make this approach effective. However, funny is hard, and this approach is clearly designed to be cute. It is easy to misfire when you approach someone this way. And depending on your value proposition, cute may be ineffective. You may come up with something clever, but you may have a very difficult time transitioning to a more substantial conversation about what you do and for whom. If you believe you have something clever that can work, test it out on a few people. Bring it to your advisory board. See what board members think. If they give you positive feedback, give it a try. Generally, however, I would avoid clever and go for a more direct description.

Let me reiterate something from Chapter 4. These descriptions should be about the benefit you deliver and not the process you use to carry it out. You don't "do college planning, research-

ing national databases to find the best higher-education values"
but rather "guide families through the college-education maze
and make sure that they pay as little as possible to the right college." It is not "we do financial planning for the suddenly single"
but "when people suddenly come into money, it is easy for them
to lose their values and make bad decisions. I show them how to
avoid those pitfalls."

If at all possible, especially in the long version of your elevator speech, make it a story rather than a description. Did you
ever wonder why so many magazine articles about an issue
don't start off with a description of the issue but start instead
with a story about someone dealing with the issue? Facts and
data are not particularly memorable. People remember stories
about people. A story about an obstacle you overcame or about
a close family member who struggled is even more powerful.

Jan, an advisor I work with, moved into the financial services business after a three-year personal struggle that involved
finances. People still ask her, "How did you make the change
from health care to financial planning?" When we started
working together, she would reply, "Well, they aren't really
that different. In health care you have nutrition and exercise
and periodic checkups, and in financial services you have bud-
geting and saving and plan reviews." I told her that she was
missing a huge opportunity to connect with people. She is
good at what she does because she cares, and she cares because
she struggled through it herself. People won't relate to a sterile
description of the process you use, I told her, they will relate to
you and what you went through. And they will appreciate why
you do it and the conviction that gives you. We eventually got
to, "I had a lot of good experiences in health care. Then I went
through a nasty three-year divorce. The trauma changed my

life. I want to make sure that no one has the same struggles I went through without someone there to help them through it. So making a career change was clear."

Consider how you communicate your value proposition. Try expressing it in shorter and longer versions. Write them out, and practice them. Try them out on different people. Finding the right words and getting comfortable with them take practice. Each time someone asks you the cocktail-party question, it is a moment of truth. It is an opportunity that you will lose if you attempt to wing it or say something a little different every time. Master it, and you will find yourself in much more productive conversations. For more exercises and tips for putting together your elevator speech, go to www.theclient drivenpractice.com/worksheets.

INCORPORATING YOUR NEW IDENTITY INTO YOUR MARKETING

If you're going to successfully own a spot on people's brains, this cannot be something you just say when meeting them at parties. It needs to be who you are. While your elevator speech is how you will introduce yourself personally, the same theme needs to run through all your marketing.

Your brochures, your website, everything you create should carry the same message. Forget about what particular expertise you represent; merely being specific will set your website apart from most financial advisors. As I mentioned earlier, most financial advisors cannot resist the urge to list everyone who might be a profitable client as someone they specialize in. In fact, I have looked at hundreds of advisor websites, and many of them don't just say the same thing—they use the same words. Make sure that your marketing communicates what's different about your clients and what's unique about what you do for them.

EFFECT ON YOUR STRATEGIC PLAN

The more thoroughly you can address the special needs of your target prospects, the more memorable you become for those prospects, and the better known you will be. The more you focus on the specific needs of your target clients, the more often people will talk about you as a specialist in those kinds of problems. And that you are the best possible advisor to talk to if a person has those problems.

Focus on your client advisory board. Make sure that it is composed, as much as possible, of people who fit the target-client description. Consider including people who advise your target clients. Ask them, "What kinds of services do you need that I should consider delivering? What would the ideal advisor for somebody like you be offering?"

It was during an advisory board session like this that I first heard a participant make the comment that he did not care about how the advisor did portfolio management. Now, I am not trying to suggest that clients of many practices feel this way. But for this practice it was true. This group was clear about what it considered important from the advisor. "Help us sort through our issues and coordinate with our other advisors. Do that, and you will get our money to manage. But don't spend our time telling us how you manage it." I bring this up because it is a good example of the surprising results you can get when you pull your target clients together. And it caused the advisor to reevaluate the services he emphasized.

See if you can solicit ideas on new services to offer. If you provide financial planning, retirement planning, asset management, and maybe insurance or estate planning and you promote no other services, it will be very difficult to differentiate yourself from other advisors. See if there are services outside these common ones that your clients might consider valuable. Offer those, and let people know that you offer them because your advisory board recommended that you do so, and it will be much easier to become known as someone who caters to your target clients' needs.

BE TRUE TO YOUR TARGET

More than anything, the focus on your target clients must be reflected in your onboarding process. You will talk with people about who you specialize in and what you do for them. When someone comes into the office to discuss becoming a client, you should be having the same conversation. You may recall from Chapter 3 the story I told about facilitating an industry think tank and discussing client onboarding processes. It was amazing to me that what advisors told me they were focusing on played no role in how they decided to accept clients. It was like they thought about a target market when they were designing their marketing strategy but ignored it once someone walked through the door. When you interview a prospective client, the first question in your mind should be, "Does this person and his or her needs fit in with the rest of my client base?" If you're going to own that piece of your clients' brains, you need to be clear with everyone you are looking to add to your practice. It should be part of your prospective client interview. Without that, it is not something you are—it is just something you say.

Being the advisor who specializes in your target clients means that you will turn away prospective clients who do not fit that profile. I discussed earlier the difference between clients you fish for and what you do with the fish that jump in the boat. You can accept some clients who do not fit the profile without necessarily jeopardizing your brand image, but it should be a clear exception. Every time you make the exception, you run the risk that more people will not recognize you as the advisor for a particular group, so think about it each time you do it. Referring prospective clients who do not fit your target profile actually can enhance your reputation within your tribe. And it can be a great opportunity to drive the message of who you are more deeply into the minds of your clients and centers of influence. I will describe more about how to capitalize on that opportunity in Chapter 7.

The same holds true for existing clients who do not fit your target market. As you grow your practice, adding more and more target clients, the legacy of clients outside your target becomes more of an issue. Beyond the marketing implications, it can be a real productivity killer.

I used to work for a high-end fee financial planning company. The company expertise was complicated, comprehensive financial plans, and we had a wealth management department that invested money into model portfolios of mutual funds. We also had an owner who could not resist the temptation to bring in any wealthy individual he could interest in a relationship. I remember one client in particular who moved over from a national brokerage firm, bringing with him a large portfolio of individual bonds. The client was retired, and generating income from his portfolio was a priority for him. He also liked the bond portfolios he had and the way they were reported by the brokerage, and he had no desire to have his portfolio managed any other way. We had no internal expertise in bonds, and our custodian's statements did not provide the client with the level of detail he wanted.

We spent a significant amount of time compensating for the mismatch between the client's expectations and our capabilities. Was all that extra work for the client worth it? No, I do not believe that it was. While the relationship was still profitable for the company, it was a distraction for the staff and periodically took us away from what we really did well. It did not position us well to extend our reputation and leverage this relationship to build more business. What kind of referral was this client going to give us, if he thought to give us any? It would not be for the services in which we excelled because that's not what he was getting from us. If he sent anyone to us, it was most likely to be other people who wanted what he wanted. Maintaining that relationship worked against our goal of generating referrals.

TARGET YOUR NETWORKING

Beyond who you decide to accept as clients, your determination of who you want to be also will tell you who you should associate with. Make it a point to get to know other people who advise the clients you specialize in. We all know that it is a good idea to network with accountants and attorneys, for example. Seek out individual specialists, and get to know them. I will talk more about that in Chapter 9.

Get to know other resources who cater to the needs of your target clients. When Mark Colgan began to specialize in clients who had recently lost a loved one, he started talking with funeral directors. He was able to be of more value to his clients by learning important information his prospective clients needed to know when making decisions during a difficult moment in their lives. The by-product, of course, was that funeral directors knew Mark as someone with a particular expertise a lot of the people they would meet probably would need.

Do you want to specialize in a certain kind of doctor? Then you probably should know insurance agents who specialize in malpractice coverage. Are your target clients people who own a specific kind of business? It would be a good idea to get to know bankers who provide services to those same kinds of entrepreneurs. Do you want to work with construction company executives? I know a company that specializes in implementing benefits plans for companies who must comply with prevailing wage laws. So should you.

This idea works in two directions. Obviously, if a lot of other professionals who work with your target market know that you are a specialist in that kind of client, there is the opportunity for them to refer to you. However, more important to your gaining ownership of that part of the center of influence's brain is that you then can be more helpful to your clients. Perhaps the most powerful way of coming to own that spot on people's brains is to become a resource to that group.

If your clients tend to have a specific collection of specialized needs (and, at some level, all well-defined target markets have at least some), and they come to find out that you can connect them with everyone they could potentially need, then you become the resource they go to. And when your clients meet other people in that target market, there is a better chance that they will refer them to you even if it is not clear that they need exactly what you do right now. They might need to meet someone who can take care of another one of their needs. If you are the person they contact to find that other resource, it is far more likely that you will see them when they have a need for your services.

BE A RESOURCE

Carol Ann Wilson is a financial planner who specializes in working with people who are going through a divorce. As you might expect, she has a significant amount of technical expertise about the financial planning aspects of that difficult life event. If you go to her website, carolannwilson.com, you will find a lot of other resources for people in such a situation. There are articles about mediation and arbitration options, courtroom dos and don'ts, and things noncustodial parents can do to stay in touch with their kids. You'll find links to the Financial Divorce Association and a website where you can find real estate divorce specialists.

It is not even terribly important that the content of your website relates to what you do. It would be good, but it is not the key concept. The important thing is that it addresses something your prospective clients find important.

Is your target market single moms? How about providing suggestions or links to resources for finding babysitters or day care? Do you work with families who have charitable foundations? Provide articles that talk about how to carry out fiduciary responsibility or communicate the importance of giving to the next generation. Trying to attract consultants with a national clientele? How about providing resources to make travel easier or better?

What organizations do your target clients belong to? Join them. Support them. If they are professional organizations, do they hold conferences? You may learn more about what that target group needs from those group meetings than you do through your client advisory board. You can learn a lot about what else your clients have access to by visiting the vendors at those conferences.

If you really want to become known as a specialist for that group of people, don't just go to the conference—speak at the conference.

Ultimately, becoming a resource makes you, as Michael Kitces describes, more referable. When you get well versed in the specific needs of your target clients, when you can be counted on to provide valuable tips and information to help those people get where they want to go, and when people know that if you cannot solve a problem for your target clients, you can connect them with someone who can, you become the person everyone in that community goes to. At that point, you have a solid hold on that part of your clients' brains. And it will be perfectly natural, when someone who knows you meets someone in your target market, for them to refer that prospect to you.

One of the most popular terms relating to the Internet and social media these days is *content marketing*. This means creating, organizing, and distributing information that your audience will find valuable. Post to your blog, write articles, create white papers, and even write books to help your target market succeed. When you start to create content and start focusing the activities of your practice on the particular solutions you deliver to target clients, you can leverage your firm's identity into powerful promotion strategies. And this is what we turn our attention to next.

CHAPTER 7

PROMOTING YOUR
NEW IDENTITY

In Chapter 6, I discussed how to be the person who represents your new value proposition. The first step in being memorable in a way that will make people want to refer you is to be the embodiment of the solution you represent to your target clients. The next step is to have a communication strategy through which you can broadcast that value proposition to the rest of the world.

The two most important aspects of your communication strategy are to be comprehensive and consistent. *Comprehensive* means that it covers any channel or medium you use, and *consistent* means that it is always the same message. Anything broadcast to the rest of the world about your practice should reinforce the message you wish to project. Anytime you (or anyone who works for you) promote the practice, you should be reinforcing the image. If your practice has a mission statement, it should address your value proposition. Your marketing collateral obviously should be consistent with the message of what solution you represent to people. Your website should discuss the same points.

Here is what I mean by comprehensive and consistent: One advisor with whom I work describes her target market as women who have been widowed within the past five years. One of the activities she does in the community that periodically brings in new clients is teaching financial courses at a local community college. Teaching adults can be a fine way to get introduced to new people. "What are the courses you teach?" I asked. "Getting your financial records organized and retirement planning," she said. The message she was delivering, the valuable content she was providing, was not aligned with her value proposition or her target market. An element of her marketing plan was not consistent with the overall identity she was attempting to promote. We worked on developing a new curriculum focused on the decisions widows have to make in the years following the loss of a spouse and what they have to do to reestablish themselves financially, and these topics will replace the courses she has been teaching. That part of her marketing plan now reinforces her reputation. The courses that she teaches are now consistent with the other public activities she has and with her overall public presence. Everything you do professionally should build on your core value proposition. Everything you do in public should add value for your target clients.

DESCRIBING YOUR NEW IDENTITY

The first challenge you may have in incorporating your new identity into your marketing plan is how to describe that identity effectively. While we have discussed the importance of having a clear target and how to create the short and long versions of your value proposition and your elevator speeches, these may not work quite as well when you move them to your website or a brochure. Sometimes it is difficult to convert something that works in conversation into marketing materials.

One thing you may need to do is reverse the order of the value proposition from the order I recommended earlier. When you are talking with people, I like the idea of making the target prospect the subject of the sentence. However, in marketing materials, this might not be particularly practical. So you will need to put what you deliver up front and make the target market the object of the sentence. For example:

- Managing the risks obstetricians and gynecologists face
- Estate planning for the multiple married
- Managing income portfolios for retirees
- Business and personal financial planning for McDonald's franchisees
- Balancing spending and saving for young families

"PRODUCTIZING" YOUR SERVICE

One effective approach is to "productize" the benefit you deliver. By this, I mean take a description of your approach, your process, or what you ultimately deliver to clients and wrap it in a package with a descriptive name. One of the challenges we face in the financial advice business is that whatever we do, even for vastly different types of client, involves many similar disciplines and strategies. As professionals, we understand the distinctions in what we are applying. But many people outside our profession have difficulty telling the difference. For example, managing a growth portfolio during the accumulation phase of a client's life and managing an income portfolio during his retirement years involve different skill sets. To most clients, however, it all looks like investment management. Estate planning involves so many different state regulations and tax codes that someone who does planning for nontraditional couples may have a knowledge base that is vastly different from that of someone who specializes in planning for couples where one partner is not a U.S. citizen. To our clients, though, it's all estate planning.

Take the various steps, emphasizing what is different about how you apply the process for your clients in particular, and give it a simple and descriptive name, and you will offer your clients and prospects a succinct way of communicating your value to people they meet.

Here are a few examples:

- The financial wellness checkup for young parents
- My 10-point portfolio risk-assessment process
- The graduate financial program for college-bound families
- The single mom's financial survival strategy
- RealLifeFinance (GersteinFisher, New York)
- Parent Care 360 (Andrew L. Comins, CLU, ChFC, MSFS)
- RetireSmart (Mass Mutual)
- Divorce Survival Kit (Carol Ann Wilson, CFDS)
- Rescue Your IRA (Brogan Financial, Knoxville, TN)

To "productize" your offering, first decide what issues it will address. Will it be oriented to risk management, college savings, retirement planning, a major life event such as the loss of a loved one or a divorce, or some aspect of investment management? Identify what you will help your clients work through and what the result will be at the end of the process.

Determine the outcomes and deliverables of your service. If it involves financial planning, decide what components of the plan will be involved. List what kinds of analyses you will perform. Decide what you will deliver and how it will look. Will it be a plan, ongoing reports, a personalized page on a website, or an analysis? Will this be something that is delivered once during your relationship with the client, or is it an ongoing service? If it is ongoing, how frequently will you deliver it to the client?

Give everything a consistent look. The plan you deliver, any ongoing reports the client receives, the worksheets you use during the process, and the marketing material to promote the process all should be named and designed so that it is clear that they belong to a cohesive system.

Once it is complete, give it a compelling name. If it is descriptive, a list-type name can work well (My 10-point . . . , My seven-step . . .). If you come up with something more like a brand name, consider having it trademarked. Whichever way you go, the point is to offer people something brief and memorable. If you have done it effectively, you can mention the name of your service to someone in your target market, and she will be intrigued enough to ask you to tell her more about it. People will not remember everything about the description of your process or the steps involved in it, but they may remember the name. Once they have that in their memory, it gives them something quick and interesting to mention to other people.

One of the benefits of "productizing" your offering is that it enables you to build trust with clients while simultaneously boosting your firm's productivity. Once you have identified the elements of your "productized" service, you can manage them to ensure that you are delivering them consistently. By explaining the elements of the process and what clients receive as a result, you are setting clear expectations. And when you consistently deliver on those expectations, you will increase client satisfaction and loyalty. Having defined each step of the process, you can manage those steps more effectively. By managing each step of the process, you have the opportunity to analyze them and execute them as efficiently as possible. A lot has been written recently about how defining and managing your processes can help to boost your profitability. With a "productized" service, you can realize efficiency gains as well as a marketing advantage.

Of course, it may be that there really is nothing entirely unique about what you do for clients. It may be that what your clients most appreciate about you is how well you do the things that all advisors must do or claim to do. In Chapter 4 I discussed attributes that do not differentiate a firm but that many advisors use as their value proposition anyway. While those aspects of your practice—good service, for example—will not differentiate your firm by themselves, you can build on those strengths to set your firm apart.

CONVERTING STRENGTHS INTO DIFFERENTIATORS: MEASURE, MANAGE, AND MASTER

To convert a strength into a differentiator, you first must be specific about what it is that you do that sets you apart. So, for example, "good service" will not differentiate you. However, if you specify what it is about your service that sets you apart, you can market that. Here are a few examples of what good service could mean:

- Returning phone calls within 24 hours
- Promptly doing what you promise you'll do
- Making sure that you have face-to-face meetings with clients at least every six months
- Following up with clients to make sure that they follow through on their responsibilities in implementing the financial plan

If you want to take this approach to set yourself apart from other advisors, I recommend a process I call *measure, manage, and master*. Let's take promptly returning phone calls as one way in which you will distinguish yourself.

Measure: Make sure that you have a system for recording when clients leave messages and when the calls get returned. You might, for example, have your receptionist make a note in your client relationship management system when a client calls instead of leaving a pink "While You Were Out" note for you. Teach your staff to make a note in the client relationship management system when they return a phone call, or program the system to automatically note it.

Manage: Regularly run a report from the system to measure how quickly calls are getting returned. Review it with your staff weekly or monthly. Discuss it in performance-evaluation meetings.

Master: Work with your staff to systematically reduce the time it takes to return calls. Encourage staff members to set aside a specific time during the day to get back to clients. Offer professional development in time management. Be creative in finding new ways to develop the skill.

Saying that you are responsive will make you sound like almost any other financial advisor and will do nothing for your marketing efforts. Being in a position to say to a prospective client, "Responsiveness is a priority for our firm. We monitor how quickly we get back to clients, and 95 percent of client phone calls are returned within 24 hours" is a position very few financial advisors are in (if only because they do not measure responsiveness) and definitely will set you apart. Find out what aspects of your service are most important to your clients, and start measuring them.

You can use measure, manage, and master with just about any customer-service issue to convert a strength into a differentiator. Do you want to be known for great follow-up? Send a letter or e-mail after each meeting or conversation with a list of your action items and the dates you anticipate their completion. Send another note when the last item is addressed. Do you want to be known for helping clients follow through on their commitments to the financial plan? David B. Yeske, CFP®, is a pioneer (maybe the creator) of *client private pages*. Each of his clients has a private web page on his site where he can post planner and client action items, each earning a checkmark on completion. The firm uses these pages to demonstrate all the things it has done for clients during their relationship and all the items clients have accomplished with the firm's guidance.

It has proven to motivate clients to follow through on tasks they need to do for themselves. "Our clients like their check-marks!" Yeske reports with a laugh.[1] I would say that Dave has mastered motivating clients to take action!

Do you want to take measure, manage, and master up a level in marketing value? "Productize" it, and call it your "Comprehensive Client Care Process" or your "Five-Point Commitment to Client Service."

CONSISTENTLY COMMUNICATE IT

Whatever strategy you choose as the basis for your com-munication plan—whether it's a truly differentiating value proposition, a branded process, or a managed commitment to customer service—this should become the focal point of your brand. Your website and brochures should feature it. Client newsletters, press releases, and blog posts should refer to it. If you want to take ownership of that spot on people's minds and stimulate referrals, it should not be *one* thing you do—it should be *the* thing you do.

Even when you speak to people about your practice, what-ever you have decided to feature should find its way into the conversation. Let's assume that you have chosen to measure, manage, and master an aspect of client service as the way you will differentiate yourself from other advisors. Your answer to the cocktail-party question should feature it: "We help corpo-rate executives organize their financial lives and make sure that they're making consistent progress on their life's goals. We're not the only ones who claim to do this, of course, so what really distinguishes us is our Comprehensive Client Care Process."

If you happen to be talking to the vice president of a publicly held company who has not been thrilled with the customer service she has received from her last two financial advisors (despite their assurances that they provide outstanding client experiences), I think there's a good chance that she will want to know more.

TEST IT FIRST

Once you have developed a course of action for your communication plan, test it with your clients before you commit to it. Bring it to your client advisory board, and present it to them. Some of the first work I do with a new advisory board is to engage them in understanding what is unique and valuable about what the advisor provides. When you have taken that feedback and used it to guide your value proposition and marketing plan, go back to them and check that what you will say about your firm to the world is what they meant. Confirm that what you will describe as the benefits clients realize by working with you are what they believe you provide. It may be that you are a little off the mark. This is when you want to go back and do some fine-tuning. Maybe you left out something that you consider a minor part of your service, and the advisory board thinks that it's important. It is possible that board members do not agree that you deliver exactly the benefits you describe. What you propose to put in all your marketing should elicit a "Yes!" from your clients before you commit to it.

As I described in Chapter 5, the board also can be valuable in reviewing your marketing materials. Pass proposed campaigns by them, and confirm that the messages connect. When you have secured your best clients' buy-in, you can be a lot more confident in rolling out your communication plan.

By the way, the feedback you receive from clients during this process is worth including in your communication plan as well. Asking is good. Telling people that you asked and what you learned about how to improve is better.

Gathering client feedback increases loyalty. Thus, when you gather feedback, make sure that your clients know that you are asking for it. You can even get some benefits from letting your prospects know.

When you do a client survey, all your clients will know about it. When you assemble a client advisory board, you can benefit from promoting that fact. Many advisors have told me that their clients and prospects are impressed when they hear about the advisory board. Just the existence of the board can be a statement of your commitment to clients.

ACTING ON FEEDBACK

Acting on feedback will push your clients closer to being engaged. The first step is to publish the results of the feedback you receive. I am not recommending that you actually distribute the full report of the survey—for many financial professionals, that's probably against compliance regulations anyway. You can, however, promote selected results. "When surveyed, my clients tell me that I consistently respond to their questions faster than they expect."

You might consider publishing a surprising result as well. "In a recent survey, you collectively gave my company newsletter a three on a scale of five. I will be looking into how I can improve it."

Include some of the results in your marketing. "I provide excellent customer service" will not differentiate you from any other advisor. Saying "When surveyed, my clients indicate that 85 percent of phone calls are returned within one business day" will.

Similarly, promote feedback from your client advisory board. Since only a few select clients can participate in the board at any one time, you may wish to have a communication plan in place to publicize the feedback. While you cannot promote specific client experiences, you can include a description of the issues discussed by the board in your company newsletters, e-mails, or posts to your website.

Indicate what you plan to do in response to the board's recommendations. Even more important, publicize the changes you make once they are in place. Changes to your office procedures, how you interact with clients, your marketing, and client events organized based on the request of the advisory board are all powerful ways to communicate that you are listening and willing to make changes to improve your clients' experience.

In *Anatomy of a Referral*, by Julie Littlechild,[2] a study revealed that 74 percent of engaged clients report that they were asked for feedback, and 72 percent believed that their feedback was important to the advisor. Communicate the feedback you've received and what actions you took in response to that feedback, and you can help get more of your clients to that coveted engaged status.

TRAIN YOUR STAFF

One opportunity I see a lot of practices miss is to engage the staff as ambassadors of the business. In many advisory firms, carrying out the marketing plan is strictly the domain of the marketing people and principals. That's a mistake.

Many advisors understand the importance of having a consistent message when describing what they do. I have seen relatively few, though, who conduct staff training on how to describe what the business does and the benefits it represents.

Effectively attracting referrals involves consistently reinforcing the description of your target prospects and the solutions or experiences you can deliver to them. Every time someone in your firm talks to the public—whether it's clients, centers of influence, or just people they meet—it is an opportunity to solidify that unique value proposition your firm represents. Your staff may interact with your clients more frequently than you do. There are probably more staff than practitioners in your firm, and so there are that many more opportunities to broadcast the message publicly if you have them all on message. Every one of those contacts contains the possibility of reinforcing your brand promise.

Sometimes your staff can be even more effective at directly stimulating referrals than you can. At an industry think tank I facilitated last year, one planner commented on how successful his paraplanners were at motivating clients to provide referrals. "There are times when I leave the room during a client meeting," he commented, "and my paraplanner will say to the client, 'We just love working with clients like you. We wish we had a hundred just like you.'" And frequently the client follows up shortly after with a referral.

More generally, however, there can be tremendous power in focusing the message across everyone in the firm. I remember working at a fee financial planning firm where the target client and value proposition were not that well defined. If you walked through the office and asked half a dozen people what the unique value and ideal client of the firm were, you'd probably get five different answers. They would be similar, but someone unfamiliar with the firm or the business might not be able to recognize that. The absence of a clear, unifying message meant that the firm would never reach a critical mass where the reputation could begin propagating itself through the community.

Another benefit to orienting the staff to your value proposition is that it provides you with a reality check. It may be that you want to go out to the world and proclaim how well you do something for clients, and your staff responds to it with, "Yeah, we don't actually do that very well." Better to know this *before* you go public with it!

While I am a big fan of involving the staff in delivering the message, I am less enthusiastic about involving them in developing the message. I have learned that while they are frequently enthusiastic ambassadors, staff members may have little interest in helping you to develop the message or little knowledge of how to describe it for marketing purposes. I used to run an organization with a team of about a dozen people who ran the spectrum of receptionist through operations personnel, managers, and ultimately, me. Several times a year I would have an off-site strategy meeting. Early on, I attempted to involve everyone in determining the priority of projects for the coming year and how we would refine or add to the services we provided. After several of these meetings, I learned through the feedback of the participants that they were not comfortable in the role of creating projects and designating priorities. In fact, a comment from one team member summarized it nicely: "Figuring out what we should be doing is what we look to you for, Steve."

I believe the same thing about your communication strategy. As the leader, you should be determining what value you deliver. A productive way of engaging the staff, however, would be to solicit stories of examples of when the practice delivered on that brand promise. Offer an idea of how you envision describing what solution or experience your firm provides to your target clients. Ask your team about their more memorable experiences of when your business carried through on its mission. Encourage a conversation about how those experiences embody what the firm does for clients. Give everyone a common reference point for talking about where they work.

CASE STUDIES

Similarly, solicit stories from clients. I discussed using your client advisory board in helping you to refine your marketing message. Engaging board members in describing how you delivered on your value proposition will help you to test and refine it. It will help you to confirm that the way you describe what you do for people is in language that clients would use themselves and will remember.

These conversations with staff and clients will accomplish more than making sure that everyone involved in your practice describes what you do the same way. They will provide you with one of the more powerful tools for communicating your value proposition—the case study.

I have said it before, and it bears repeating in the context of developing an overall communication strategy—people don't remember features and benefits, and people often will not remember your value proposition or deliverables, but people do remember stories about people. And those stories can be an incredibly efficient means of communicating an intangible collection of benefits in a memorable way.

Use these case studies as a basis for how you will systematically communicate what you do. I will talk about a number of different tools and strategies to help establish and build your reputation and attract referrals. Many of these methods can use the case study as a foundation for delivering your message. What makes these vignettes so effective is that they combine the power of storytelling with a focus on the good outcomes you produce, the benefits you deliver.

David Meerman Scott, in his book *World Wide Rave*, discusses many strategies for creating excitement about what you do. One of the fundamental concepts in creating a rave is to talk about the good things that happened to people who used your service. "Never talk about your products and services again," he says. "Instead, focus on your buyer personas and how you can solve problems for them."[3] Be careful to avoid testimonials and use general or composite hypothetical examples.

Case studies also will help you to avoid a mistake I have mentioned that bears repeating: In your communication strategy, you need to be talking about the solutions you deliver and not the process you use to get there. As Scott Degraffenreid says repeatedly in his book, *Embracing the N.u.d.e. Model: The New Art and Science of Referral Marketing*, "Nobody gives a crap about process."[4]

Feature these case studies in your brochures and on your website. Make a habit of collecting them at staff meetings so that you can feature a different one periodically on your blog or each time you send out a client newsletter. Replace the tedious listings of the services you provide with these stories. For more information on how to put together a case study for your practice, go to www.theclientdrivenpractice.com/case-study.

BE THE EXPERT

What else can you do to promote your new identity? In Chapter 6, I suggested that you become a resource for your target clients. To better broadcast your new reputation, take it a step further and be an expert. Becoming known as *the* person to go to when the target client needs a particular kind of solution is the ultimate in niche marketing.

Study more about the particular needs and circumstances of your target clients. Become a student of them, and publish what you find—blog posts, articles, white papers, e-books, and even books. Conduct client education events or seminars, and speak at meetings or conferences where your target clients gather. Find opportunities to communicate with your target clients about how they can solve their problems.

Remember attorney Rob Brown from Chapter 4? He has developed that level of expertise and built his reputation in the solution that he provides. As a result, people come to him. It is the pinnacle of referral marketing. In addition to attracting incoming calls, being positioned as an expert will help you to close cases.

Anthony Gallea is managing director of the Pelican Bay Group—a producer group with Morgan Stanley Smith Barney. Earlier in his career, Tony's target market was people moving into retirement, especially from one large local employer. He, like an awful lot of financial advisors, wanted to catch people at that particular time in the hope of having an opportunity to manage their individual retirement account (IRA) rollover, if that was the option appropriate for them. In targeting that population, however, he did something that very few other financial advisors did—he literally wrote the book on how to do it. *The Lump Sum Handbook*[5] addressed all the various issues retirees would have to work through in taking distributions from their retirement plans. When an employee contemplating retirement interviewed half a dozen financial advisors, Tony could say, "Listen, whatever you decide, I want you to have a copy of the most recent edition of my book. It may be helpful regardless of which direction you decide to go in." Who do you think that person was going to hire?

Key to this strategy is to communicate with your target prospects about what can be done to solve their problems, not what *you* can do to solve their problems. Share with people tips and ideas about how they can get where they want to go, and you're an expert; tell people what you can do for them, and you're a salesperson. Of course, you want to be talking about ideas related to the services you provide, but, as David Meerman Scott points out, they should be *tied to* and not *touting* what clients can hire you for.

The fundamental concept of this communication plan within your referral marketing strategy is reputation marketing rather than traditional firm marketing. I focused my attention with advisors on driving referrals in part because in my opinion it is the only kind of marketing with a worthwhile return on investment. Advertising, direct mail, and even public relations—none of these work unless you can conduct them on a huge scale. You are not Ameriprise or Merrill Lynch (they will get special editions of this book). You cannot afford to buy the rights to Snoopy, as Metropolitan Life did. It takes massive capital to push your image onto prospective clients. You need to build a reputation that works its way organically through the community you wish to serve. Fortunately, in these days of the Internet, social media, and electronic communication, it is possible for even a small firm to promote its expertise successfully to a target population.

Once you have a clear idea of who you want to serve and the solution or experience they're looking for, work to build expertise in that area and create opportunities to share that expertise.

We have discussed becoming the person who provides target clients with the solutions they seek and how to communicate with the world your expertise in being that person. Let's now bring it back to the individual client level and discuss how to conduct the new referral conversation with clients.

CHAPTER 8

THE NEW REFERRAL CONVERSATION

I have said many times that it's a bad idea to ask for referrals. Let me clarify this a little bit. What I really object to is using some form of the "Who do you know?" question. Attempting to attract clients with this question is disrespectful of the natural process that leads to referrals and puts the client on the spot. It is a closed-end question that makes clients feel bad if they must honestly respond, "No one." This question serves *our* purposes and not the client's. However, this doesn't mean that we shouldn't speak with our clients about referrals. It means that with the benefit of the research we now have, we need to approach the discussion in a different way. It means that we need a new referral conversation.

If clients are predisposed to helping us, and most of them are, how can we bring up the topic in such a way that if they can't think of anyone to recommend to us, they don't feel put on the spot? Can we ask for a favor in a way that doesn't require that they do the prospecting for us? Can we ask for assistance in a way that does not run the risk of their betraying one of their friendships?

We can stimulate referrals to happen naturally if we can own a particular spot on the client's brain. So how can we talk about referrals in such a way that it advances our ownership over that cerebral real estate? One fundamental aspect of this approach is to engage clients' creativity. If we ask them a question with a simple yes or no answer, they will either be able to produce a quick response or they won't. It doesn't take us any further. However, if we ask them some kind of open-ended question, we can get them thinking about something. Even if they just consider it for a little while, we probably have engaged them on a deeper level. Engage their creativity, and you will make a deeper impression.

The new referral conversation is about interacting with our clients the way friends would interact with each other or enlisting their help in solving a problem. Whatever approach we take, it should be a conversation that delivers benefits to the client.

TRIGGER PHRASES

One aspect of the new referral conversation is that it can grow naturally out of educating the client. You have worked hard to determine who are your ideal clients, what problems they have, and what kinds of solutions or experiences they seek. Ideally, you have reviewed your service mix and made some adjustments to tailor it more closely to those ideal clients. So the natural place for the new referral conversation to begin is with a description of the problem you have decided to focus on solving or the need you have determined to fill. By extension, you will be drawing a picture for your clients of your ideal prospect. Your objective is to identify and reinforce expressions that will prompt your clients to mention you. You want to teach your clients how to recognize a great referral.

In his book, *The Referral Engine*, John Jantsch says, "I believe any salesperson worth their salt has developed a list of phrases, situations, and verbal clues that, if heard during a sales presentation, signal it's time to take the order. The same idea is true of a qualified referral."[1]

What are your trigger phrases?

- I was just awarded another allocation of stock options, and I'm not sure exactly what they can do for me.
- My company just moved to a cash-balance retirement plan.
- My best friend's husband was just diagnosed with Alzheimer's disease.
- We went to my son's high school last night to hear the guidance counselor talk about financial aid.
- My sister just had her first child.

Take some time to talk with your clients about who you have realized your ideal clients are. And discuss those ideal clients in terms of needs they might express that you are particularly good at fulfilling. Teach your clients those trigger phrases so that when they hear them again, you will pop into their mind.

"We are focusing all our attention on helping small businesses design effective retirement plans, especially to make sure that they comply with the new regulations. If you hear someone you know who owns a business talk about all these confusing mailings they are getting from their retirement plan provider, and they can't figure out what to do about it, I would love an introduction. I can probably be a big help to them, like I was to you."

Whenever you speak to people, you should be talking about the solution or experience you represent. People benefit from making a referral when they can introduce someone they know to someone who can provide them with something they want or need. Sprinkling these trigger phrases throughout your conversations teaches people how they can help one of their friends by mentioning you. Repetition is the mother of instruction, so look for opportunities to mention these trigger phrases again and again. People make referrals because they believe they can help somebody, because they can improve their standing among their peers by making introductions to resources that will solve the problems their friends are experiencing. Consistently teaching your clients those trigger phrases will help to prepare them to recognize an opportunity to connect something a friend said to a resource that can address the problem. For more help on discovering the right trigger phrases to use with clients, go to www.theclientdrivenpractice.com/trigger-phrases.

DON'T ASK FOR REFERRALS— ASK FOR INTRODUCTIONS

Beyond teaching clients the key phrases to listen for, you can still ask for referrals. You just have to learn how to do it in a different way. Clients generally are willing to introduce you to other people (at least 93 percent of them, according to Julie Littlechild[2]). The problem with the "Who do you know?"

question is that you are asking your clients to do too much of the work for you and to take the chance that the people they send to you actually have a financial problem they are looking for someone to solve. Making the introduction is not typically the biggest cause of discomfort when you ask for a referral; it is all the assumptions clients have to make to decide whether someone needs to be introduced to you. Not to mention the fact that you typically ask them on the fly, without giving them the benefit of considering it or doing homework, even if they are predisposed to do so.

So don't ask for referrals—ask for introductions. Do your homework, and identify people who can benefit from the unique value you represent. Figure out which of them has some connection to a client, and then ask your client if she would be willing to introduce you. A simple introduction is an easy and comfortable way for a client to help you. You are not asking the client to make an assessment, from among all the people she may know, about who might benefit from what you can do. You already know. All you need is to be introduced.

This removes a significant amount of risk from the transaction for the client. You will not be calling the prospect and saying, "Samantha is a client, and she suggested that you might benefit from my services." Instead, Samantha will call your prospect and say something like, "Steve has been doing some really good work to help me with [describe the financial issue you specialize in] and told me that he thinks you could benefit from the work he does as well. He asked if I might introduce the two of you. Would you be willing to take his call?"

You are not asking Samantha to evaluate her friend and determine that he needs someone like you. You are not asking Samantha to tell you anything about her friend, specifically about his finances. Most important, you are not asking Samantha to figure out who your prospects are. Samantha knows someone you would like to meet, and you are asking her for a simple introduction.

The obvious question is, Who should you ask to be introduced to? This gets to the heart of the issue. When you ask a client the "Who do you know?" question, you are asking him to prospect for you. It's not the client's job to prospect for you. It's one thing to ask a client to be willing to make a referral; it's quite another to ask a client to do your homework.

If you are diligent at implementing the ideas in this book, you will be enhancing the natural way that referrals happen, and clients will benefit from being prepared for the opportunity to refer you. The need to ask for referrals will be decreased. Decreased, but probably not eliminated. And at least until your reputation for providing a unique benefit is established and makes its way through the community, you will still need to ask for your clients' help. Asking them to do you a favor by introducing you to someone else is reasonable; asking them to do your job is not. So don't ask for referrals—ask for introductions.

Who should you ask to be introduced to? Well, that's where the homework comes in. You probably know a fair amount about your clients, and this information can lead to discovering people they might know who could benefit from hiring you. What kind of information are we talking about? Their profession, employer, professional organization, faith community, social organization, and country club—and any other tribes to which your clients may belong. Whatever makes the client part of your target market will give you significant clues about who else he may be able to introduce you to. Do you work with chiropractors? They have professional associations. University professors? Find out who else works at that college. Are your clients Rotarians? Look up other members of the chapter.

There are many ways to find other people in the communities your clients belong to. Country clubs and professional organizations have directories. Many professions are licensed through the government, and their licenses are public record. Of course, the game changer in the past 10 years has been the Internet. It used to require a fair amount of legwork to come up with the names of people your clients were connected to. That is no longer true, thanks to the web.

USING LINKEDIN TO GET INTRODUCED

Sam Richter has done the most thorough and creative work I have seen on researching people and connections on the web. When I attend his presentations, I cannot possibly write fast enough to take all the notes I want to. His book, *Take the Cold Out of Cold Calling*,[3] is a must-read. I will review one strategy I learned from him—how to use LinkedIn to find people to be introduced to.

LinkedIn is a social networking website, a sort of professional version of Facebook. It is a way for people to connect with each other professionally. You can establish an account and input your professional information and your résumé. You can connect with people you know socially and people with whom you do business. You can join discussion groups on hundreds of topics. If you have a problem you need solved, you can post a question to LinkedIn Answers, and experts in that professional area can post suggestions. The most powerful aspect of LinkedIn for finding new prospects is the visibility of other peoples' networks. If you connect with people, meaning that you invite them to connect with you and they accept, you can then see everyone with whom they are connected.

Chances are there's enough information in a LinkedIn profile to give you a pretty good idea of whether that person is in your target market. Here's how to make use of that to get introduced to new clients. Connect with as many of your clients as you can find on LinkedIn. Before you go to a meeting with one of those clients, take a look at the people they're connected to. Chances are that you can find at least a couple of potential candidates for your services among them. When you meet with your client, ask for an introduction.

Reinforce the description of your target client, remind your client of the solution you represent, and mention that you know a little bit about the candidate you identified. Explain why you believe that he could benefit from the services you provide. Tell your client that you noticed that he was connected to his friend on LinkedIn, and ask if he would do the favor of introducing you to him.

This is fundamentally different from the "Who do you know?" question. You are not asking your client to suggest which of his friends and acquaintances could be candidates for your services. You are telling your client who you believe would be a good candidate based on what you have found out about him. All you are asking for is an introduction. Of course, there are reasons your client may not want to make the introduction, and there are graceful ways for him to say no. ("I really don't know him well at all, and he does not know me well enough for an introduction to get you anywhere.") However, it is more likely that your client will be happy to help and will respond positively.

Let me take just a moment to address the compliance questions I often get about using social media. The beauty of this strategy is that it does not trigger any compliance requirements. If you have a securities license, the one compliance approval you will need to get is to have a LinkedIn profile in the first place. But even the wire houses are allowing their brokers and advisors to have profiles. Most of what is regulated is what you post to LinkedIn. Identifying prospects to be connected to is strictly research. There are no regulations I know of that limit what you can glean from a public website. So there are no compliance restrictions against looking at the profiles of the people who are connected to your clients.

Beyond asking for introductions, there are other ways you can engage your clients' creativity in helping to connect you with new prospects. Rather than asking them for the names of people you should contact, ask for their advice and guidance.

DON'T ASK FOR REFERRALS—
ASK FOR ADVICE

Let me introduce you to the most powerful business-building question I ever learned. The question was taught to me by Bruce Peters, my coach and mentor and my predecessor in doing client advisory boards for financial advisors. I have used it in many scenarios regarding many services. I have used it in sales presentations and performance evaluations. I frequently ask it on behalf of advisors at their client advisory board meetings. It is a powerful question: "If you were in my position, trying to do what I am trying to accomplish, what would you do?"

Let's examine the value of this question in the context of getting referrals. People feel complimented when they are asked for advice. Remember why people make referrals? Because it improves their standing in the eyes of their peers. Asking for their advice shows your respect for your clients and enables them to do something to elevate it further. It gets their creative juices flowing. It elicits the kind of information you want while strengthening the relationship rather than diminishing it, which is what happens when you ask directly for referrals.

For example, how does a typical client feel when asked, "Who do you know who can use my services?" Now, compare that to how you suppose the client would feel if, after providing a description of your target client, you ask, "If you were looking for other people like this, what would you do?"

First, this puts a lot more context around the request. It is a lot easier to recall people of a certain description than it is to think of people "who could potentially use your services." It engages your client's creativity. If anyone comes to mind, there's a good chance that your client will offer her name. If not, the client has a graceful way out. There is no wrong answer. You even may get some good marketing ideas from your client.

As I mentioned earlier, this question can be used in all kinds of situations: If you had to describe the value of these services to other people like you, what would you say? If you were trying to provide the ideal services to business owners such as yourself, what services would you offer? If you were trying to connect with your trade association, how would you do it? If you had to fill the position of receptionist, as I do, where would you look to find the best candidate? If you were trying to improve your performance in this one particular area, what do you suppose you would try first?

Asking your clients to be creative may trigger an idea to introduce you to someone specific without your asking for that name specifically. If, for example, you work with corporate executives, you might know that one of the trigger expressions is the awarding of stock options. If you ask your client, "What other kinds of scenarios do you think I should be asking about to find people like that?" your client may respond with something like, "Well, the obvious thing would be to ask if anyone was just promoted to the level of senior vice president because in our company that's where those kinds of benefits kick in." And this might be quickly followed by, "Oh! That reminds me—my friend Josh was just promoted to that level. You should give him a call."

Another benefit of this strategy, besides not putting clients on the spot, is that it gets them thinking about how to communicate the benefits of your service to other people and identifying situations where you would offer the most value. The more you get them to think about it, the more neurons you can involve that connect you with particular scenarios that you hope will trigger a referral. The more you get their brain working on that problem, the more likely it is that they will remember to mention you when the right opportunity arises. Do this consistently enough and you will find more of your clients giving your name to the qualified prospects they bump into.

LEVERAGING THE "BAD" REFERRAL

Another teaching scenario comes masqueraded as a problem. Have you ever had a really good client refer you to someone who is totally wrong for your practice? Of course you have—

we all have. And you feel like you have to take that referral as a client because if you don't, you will be insulting the great client who referred him, and that will be the end of any referrals from that great client. Right? Wrong!

You don't have to accept the referral of someone who is outside your target market. What you need to do is honor the referral that you receive, and there are other ways of doing that besides taking a client who does not fit your practice. Here is what to do: Of course, you will meet with the person who was referred by your great client. Once you recognize that it would be a poor fit, explain this to the prospect. Describe your ideal client and the particular solution or experience you provide, communicating how that solution has been tailored to your target client, the fact that you have focused your practice on that kind of client, and that those are the only kinds of clients you are currently accepting. Then help the person find a more appropriate advisor. "I've been in this business a long time, and I've come to know many of the financial professionals in town. I am sure that once I think about it, I will be able to recommend three or four other advisors who have practices better suited to your needs. Let me do a little research and get you their contact information."

And then make sure that you follow through! You don't have to bring that person in as a client, but you do have to honor the referral.

And by the way—you have just educated another person about your ideal client and the solution you provide. Assuming that you have followed through and treated the referral well, you have just created another person who can provide you with referrals.

Once you have gotten the list to the prospective client, call the client who made the referral. Start by thanking him for recommending you. Let him know how much that shows he trusts you and how honored you are to have that level of trust. Then tell the client what you did. "When I interviewed your friend, I realized that he is not looking for the particular kind of solution I have focused my practice on and that it would be a poor fit. However, I know a lot of the financial practitioners in town, so I composed a list of other advisors whose practices better suit him. I sent your friend their contact information and offered to make introductions if that would be helpful."

Then explain to your client the particular solution you have focused your practice on, the description of the ideal client, and maybe some of the trigger phrases that would help your client to recognize an ideal person to refer to you.

Who do you suppose is the most likely person to do you a favor? Someone you have done a favor for? This would be a reasonable assumption. Interestingly, though, the most likely person to do you a favor is someone who has done you a favor before. Doing favors for you leads people to like you more and increases the likelihood that they would want to do you another favor. Sometimes referred to as the *Ben Franklin effect* because the founding father documented using this approach for his own benefit, it has since been verified by research.[4] The same thing is most likely true about referrals. The most likely clients to make referrals to you are the ones who have done so in the past. As long as you honor the referral and take good care of the person your client refers to you, which may mean directing that person to someone more appropriate, it is likely that the client will continue to refer to you.

And if you end up sending that referral to another practitioner, it gives you the opportunity to reinforce with your client the particular solution you represent and your ideal client. Repeat, repeat, repeat. Every opportunity you have to reinforce that message advances your ownership of that part of your client's brain. Receiving a referral of someone who is not right for your practice can be just as profitable as getting a new client. The likelihood that the referrer will send you other people is increased, and you have an opportunity to reiterate a description of the kinds of people you are hoping to find. A "bad" referral can be a very positive thing.

You need to talk with your clients about referrals. And you need to have those conversations in a way that respects the natural process that generates referrals. You need to understand the benefits clients receive when they make a good recommendation to a friend. If sending the right person to you to get what you provide helps your client to improve his standing among his peers, if it extends his influence and enables him to be seen as a source of solutions himself, then it will be in his best interest to mention you when the opportunity arises. Practice and master the new referral conversation, and you will find that talking with your clients about referrals will be a positive experience for both of you.

However, clients are not the only people you need to have a new referral conversation with. The other audience for this discussion is centers of influence.

CHAPTER 9

CENTERS OF INFLUENCE

So far we've discussed creating an identity associated with something that our target clients are looking for and systematically communicating it so that we can own that piece of the client's brain. The more closely identified we become with a certain solution or experience, the more likely it is that our clients will remember it when they hear those trigger phrases that identify a good referral, and the more likely they will be to refer us when the opportunity arises. There is another audience for us to communicate that identity to, and it bears a separate piece of the discussion. That audience is centers of influence.

Attracting referrals from centers of influence is similar to attracting referrals from clients. The opportunity, though, is much larger. While our clients may regularly bump into target prospects, the right centers of influence will come into contact with them daily. Further, while people gladly accept recommendations from their friends, centers of influence are typically advisors to those target prospects—people from whom they are actively seeking recommendations. Centers of influence, then, hold the potential of referring many more motivated target clients.

While attracting referrals from centers of influence follows many of the same principles as attracting referrals from clients, there are some significant differences that must be taken into account when developing a referral marketing strategy aimed at those other professionals. Probably the most significant difference is the motivation that drives the referral in the first place. Your clients, friends, and acquaintances make referrals as social currency—to increase their standing among their peers and to do favors for people they care about. Centers of influence are in professional relationships with people they would potentially refer and have ethical and professional responsibilities to those people. Accountants and attorneys, in particular, most commonly will have as their top concern and among their top motivations how well their clients' needs will be addressed and how they will be serviced. Your clients will recommend you to their friends because they had a good experience; a professional will recommend you to his clients only if he has a belief, based on evidence, that your skills can effectively address his clients' needs. Therefore, while your primary objective in developing a referral marketing strategy for clients is to systematically reinforce the solution or experience you provide and to teach your clients the trigger phrases that let them know someone needs what you do, your goals in developing a referral strategy with centers of influence must go beyond simply identifying the experience you deliver. It must demonstrate more thoroughly your skills at delivering that solution.

Beyond that, centers of influence also will ask the basic question that every prospect has on her mind: What's in it for me? When you meet a prospective client, what's in it for that person is a solution that addresses the need she perceives. When a client refers someone to you, what's in it for her is elevation in social standing. With centers of influence, what's in it for them is how well their clients will be taken care of (as I discussed earlier) and whether you can help them build their businesses. If you can demonstrate that your technical abilities and service model will make sure that the clients' needs are addressed effectively, and you can assist the clients in building their own businesses, you have the keys to attracting a stream of referrals from other professionals.

RECIPROCITY

When I see advisors fail in their attempts to attract referrals from other professionals, one of those two issues typically has been addressed poorly. I can think of many conversations with advisors who are frustrated because, although they were sending new clients regularly to the center of influence, they were not getting any referrals in return. I remember clearly a conversation I had with an advisor recently who was describing his challenges in stimulating referrals from centers of influence. "They just don't seem to get the reciprocity thing," he said. Well, that would be correct. They won't send their clients to you simply to return a favor. They are keenly aware of their ethical and professional responsibilities to those clients. As our industry moves more in the direction of a fiduciary standard, I anticipate that I will hear comments like that less frequently. Accountants and attorneys especially will care first and foremost about how well their clients' needs will be addressed and whether they will receive dependable, professional, and excellent service. No amount of desire to return a favor to a referral will trump those concerns. Rapport with potential referrers is important, but the practice of developing rapport and sending a few people their way will not be the right approach to attracting clients from other professionals. Most accountants and attorneys will not make referrals simply to be reciprocal. First, you need to make it clear that a client of theirs who fits your target profile *needs* to come to you for something that you are uniquely in a position to provide.

Once they are satisfied that your business delivers something that their clients need, many centers of influence will be open to engaging you to assist them in building their businesses. Providing a positive client experience may not be enough. I have spoken with many advisors who provide an excellent client experience and who have demonstrated to centers of influence that they treat clients very well, and still they don't get referrals. Once you are over the hurdle of demonstrating to a potential referrer that her clients would benefit from working with you, being attentive to assisting them in building their businesses is the second element. Fulfilling both those requirements—proving that their clients need something you do and showing them that you want to help them build their businesses—will make your referral marketing strategy effective.

LEVERAGING EXISTING CLIENT RELATIONSHIPS

With that in mind, how do you proceed? The challenge is to get connected to potential centers of influence and to demonstrate your expertise and your level of service over a long enough period of time for them to come to understand that that's normal practice for us. How do we find a scenario where we can get in front of them and be in touch consistently enough to accomplish this? The most obvious place to start is with the other advisors of your current clients. In addition to cultivating potential centers of influence, you also can perform an important service for your clients.

There was a discussion in a client advisory board I facilitated recently of an issue I have heard before. This was a meeting for a financial planning practice. One of the participants, a busy and successful small-business leader, commented, "The best thing you can do for me is to coordinate my other advisors. I have a lot of complicated things going on, and it's difficult for me to put together all the advice I'm getting from the other accountants and attorneys." The client clearly placed a significant value on the planner's willingness to coordinate the various aspects of his financial plan. Of course, if you do this for a client, you will necessarily be speaking on a fairly regular basis with the client's accountants and attorneys. Forget about telling potential referral sources how good your service is; demonstrate it by coordinating the efforts of the client's advisors. In addition to making a favorable impression on the accountants and attorneys you end up working with, you also will be increasing client loyalty.

DON'T ASK FOR REFERRALS— ASK FOR ADVICE

When you're working to attract referrals from clients, I have recommended that you not ask for referrals but rather ask for advice. You can ask the same question of people who also advise your target clients. "Knowing what I am attempting to help people with, if you were in my position, what would you do?" When you ask this question of a client, one of the outcomes you are hoping for is that you will trigger the memory of a person she can refer to you. The same holds true for centers of influence. However, the person you're talking to is probably trying to attract many of the same kinds of clients. He may share with you some of his more successful strategies for attracting those clients. Regardless, you are engaging his creativity in the same way you are involving your client's creativity. Get his brain working on the problem, and it is more than likely that he'll remember you when a client walks through the door expressing a need for the kind of thing you do.

DON'T ASK FOR REFERRALS— ASK WHO YOU CAN REFER

There is another, related question that can be even more effective with centers of influence. Rather than asking who they can refer to you, ask who you can refer to them. It gives you an opportunity to describe your ideal client and the solution you represent, and it demonstrates that you can be of value in building their business. "People like [describe your target prospect] come to me for [solution you represent]. So, in working with those people, it is pretty common that they need the assistance of other advisors as well. I always like to have a list of people I can recommend when that happens. Will you describe for me your ideal client so that I can recognize the right people to recommend to you?"

This accomplishes a few things. It gives you the opportunity to describe what kind of solution or experience you represent in the context of information giving rather than selling. It keeps you from having to ask for referrals, which almost always causes the other advisor to immediately raise the barricades for the rest of the conversation. And it demonstrates that you can be an asset to him in helping to build his business.

It also gives you an opportunity to discuss in detail what the center of influence does in his practice. Investing time to find out about his practice develops rapport and gives you a reason to have ongoing interaction. That interaction can begin with your mutual client.

So often I see financial planners, investment advisors, accountants, attorneys, and other client advisors working in their own professional area, never collaborating with professionals from other disciplines. Much of what we do has implications in the disciplines of our clients' other advisors. Reaching out and collaborating can help to build professional relationships that turn into referral relationships. You might even pick up a couple of good ideas for your clients.

What would happen if you picked up the phone and called the client's accountant and said, "I have been working on our mutual client's retirement plan, and I have been considering recommending a Roth IRA conversion. Here's what I see as the advantages and disadvantages. What would you see as the pros and cons?" In doing advisory boards, I frequently tell advisors who are unsure about what will come from the process that only good things can come from gathering some of your best clients in a room and asking them how you can improve your service to them. I feel the same way about our clients' other advisors. If we make a habit of building relationships with the other people on the client's team, I can see only good things coming from it.

Asking a center of influence for her opinion can be a lot more than bouncing your ideas off her. Other professionals are often sensitive when they perceive that another advisor is offering recommendations in their area of specialty. I have spoken with a lot of estate attorneys, for example, who have made it clear that they do not appreciate it when a financial advisor recommends a specific estate planning device. Why not act like a team on behalf of the client? When working on an estate case, why not call the client's attorney and say, "I have been working on this issue for our mutual client. I have a couple of ideas about how this could be approached, but how do you think it should be addressed?"

For that matter, you could meet with the other advisor (with your client's permission, of course; this is going to generate an invoice for the client) and review with her the plan you have developed for the client. Find out what she sees as weaknesses or areas that have not been addressed. It is a valuable collaboration for the client, it generates billable hours for the other professional, and it gives you an opportunity to demonstrate the quality of your work to someone who potentially could be sending you referrals. Everybody wins.

CENTERS OF INFLUENCE ON THE ADVISORY BOARD

Getting feedback from centers of influence does not have to be limited to individual cases. If they work with a lot of people who are in your target market, their feedback on what services to provide and how to structure your practice can be invaluable. Involving them in tailoring the client experience can help to give them a sense of ownership and increase their confidence when they contemplate referring a client to you. And if a center of influence provides you with consistent referrals already, it would be a great idea to involve him in any systematic gathering of feedback that you do. I work with one advisor who gets a significant portion of her new business from an accounting practice with whom she has close ties. I work with another wealth management firm that gets a consistent stream of referrals from an influential local estate attorney. You'd better believe both those centers of influence are on the advisors' client advisory boards.

The guidance you can get by having a center of influence on your advisory board can be invaluable, and there's more. You can spend a lot of time telling centers of influence how satisfied and loyal your clients are, but when they hear it directly from those clients in their own words, as often happens in advisory board meetings, it can make a much more significant impression. In our business, we cannot use testimonials in our marketing. Having the same kinds of comments come up spontaneously in discussion is both compliant and much more powerful.

There are some situations where convening an advisory board or focus group comprised entirely of centers of influence and potential centers of influence can be very effective. I worked with an advisor who was developing a service that naturally dovetailed with estate planning. We believed that there was a natural link between this advice and what the client then would work on with his attorney. So it seemed natural to explore whether those practitioners saw the same kind of fit and what kinds of advice they would have for us. What could we do in our engagement to help better prepare the clients for when they went to their attorney? Where did those attorneys see the line between what we intended to do and where their discipline began? So we convened an advisory board of estate attorneys, and it went remarkably well. The attorneys were interested and engaged in the conversation from the beginning. They had a lot of really good guidance about what we could discuss and discover that would help them, things clients frequently don't want to talk about with their attorneys because they don't want to use billable hours to do it. They told us which areas to avoid because they saw those conversations as more appropriate for the attorney. As a result, the advisor got a lot of good advice on the development of service and actually began developing a couple of potential referral relationships before we even left.

SHARING SURVEY RESULTS

In addition to getting feedback from other practitioners, we can offer them our feedback as well. Julie Littlechild and her company, Advisor Impact, have included in their client surveys questions about the clients' other advisors. In teaching advisors how to use the results of the surveys, the company uses the feedback on clients' other advisors as a way to get introduced to them. The company's recommended process includes contacting the other professionals to learn more about their practices so that they can make better referrals to them.

Advisor Impact also recommends taking the feedback on those other advisors and letting them know about it. "We just did a client survey and asked our clients to rate all their advisors. I thought you might like to know what the clients had to say about you." This is a great way to break the ice! And it's a good way to build rapport and a relationship with them by sharing information that may help them provide better service to their clients.

Gathering this kind of feedback also can be very valuable after you have referred someone to another professional. A little while after you introduce a client, perhaps two or three months, contact the client to see how happy she is with the referral you offered her. Ask permission to share those comments with the other advisor. You are then in a position to thank the other advisor for the great job he is doing or to offer feedback that could help the other advisor improve his client experience.

HARVESTING COMPLAINTS

Speaking of client feedback, centers of influence hear bad as well as good comments from clients about the other professionals with whom they work, just as, I am sure, you do. Planting the seed with a center of influence to remember you when one of her client's other relationships goes bad is referred to by global private wealth expert Russ Alan Prince as *harvesting complaints*.[1] One of the major obstacles we face in attracting referrals from other professionals is that most of their clients are already receiving financial advice from someone else. Over the course of time, however, relationships change, investment strategies fail, and other advisors may not continue to evolve while the environment (and client expectations) moves forward. Including expressions of dissatisfaction in the trigger phrases you share with centers of influence can help you to capture these opportunities.

THE WRONG REFERRAL

Referrals who do not fit your target-client profile are another opportunity to strengthen the referral relationship with the center of influence in much the same way poor referrals from clients can be an opportunity. Handle them similarly to a referral from a client: Explain to the prospect the mismatch, offer to help her find a more suitable advisor, direct her to several people to choose from, follow up with your center of influence to explain what you did, and use the opportunity to reinforce your description of your ideal client and the particular value you bring to a situation. One difference you may consider incorporating for referrals from other professionals is to send the center of influence the list of alternative advisors you plan to recommend before you send it to the prospective client. Remember, the center of influence is most concerned with the welfare of the client he sent to you. While he will appreciate your recognition that you are not the best candidate to assist the client with a particular issue, he may have opinions about or need background information on the other people you recommend. He may have other people he can recommend to the client if you are not the right person, and more important, he may have a list of people he specifically would *not* want his client to go to.

COMMUNICATION STRATEGIES AND JOINT WORK

A communication strategy directed at centers of influence can work both ways. You can include centers of influence on the distribution list for your blog posts or newsletters. There may be useful information for those other professionals if they deal with the same kinds of clients you do. Regardless, it is an opportunity to provide, on an ongoing basis, reminders of your expertise. The centers of influence even can participate in this strategy as well. Ask other professionals for articles or guest posts. This provides the dual benefits of delivering to your clients valuable information from other disciplines while giving the other professionals an opportunity to get introduced to potential new clients of their own.

In helping you to develop your communication strategy, I have recommended delivering talks and writing articles relevant to your target market. Invite centers of influence to work with you on projects such as these. Joint projects can lead to joint clients. Cooperating on the manuscript for an article or working together on researching a white paper helps to reinforce your expertise and develop a relationship. As you hone your skills in publishing and speaking to build your business, you can benefit centers of influence by sharing that expertise and showing them how it can build their practices as well. Involving them in your public-relations efforts can be of tremendous benefit.

If you have not identified opportunities to give presentations where you can cooperate with centers of influence, create them. Emerson Investment Management of Boston periodically holds "summits" that bring together professionals from several firms to address a common topic. Each of the firms involved invites its clients and encourages its clients to bring friends. The evening meetings may address an investment management idea, an estate planning topic, or a financial planning issue. All the firms involved contribute, and all the firms benefit.

It is probably not practical to pursue all these methods of attracting referrals from centers of influence. I'm not implying that your strategy should include them all. I'm laying out the different possibilities for two reasons: to give you a bunch of ideas in the hope that you will pursue one or a couple and to show you how considering the needs of centers of influence can lead to different ways to build relationships with them that can result in referrals.

Ultimately, whatever you can do to be in regular contact with centers of influence, to demonstrate to them your expertise and to help them understand that referring target clients to you is the best thing for the clients, and to help them build their businesses are activities worth considering in your professional referral marketing strategy. While their perspective and their motivations are somewhat different from those of clients who may refer to you, the basic principles of referral marketing still apply. Understand how a center of influence benefits from referring a client to you, and provide that benefit to him. Systematically communicate the solution or experience you represent, your ideal client, and your particular skills and expertise. Share the trigger phrases that would indicate that someone needs what you provide, and find ongoing opportunities to consistently communicate them to centers of influence so that you can gradually take ownership of that spot on their brains.

Centers of influence represent a significant opportunity for business development because they come in contact with so many prospective clients and their recommendation generally carries more weight than a friend's or acquaintance's suggestion. Draft your strategy with these principles in mind, and other professionals can play a major role in your business-development efforts.

CHAPTER 10

YOUR REFERRAL MARKETING STRATEGY

There are a lot of concepts in this book that will help you to attract consistent referrals. But as with your clients' finances, all the concepts you marshal on their behalf can't do the most good until they are brought together into a cohesive strategy. This is what I will talk about here.

IDENTIFYING YOUR TARGET MARKET

The first step in creating your plan is to identify who you want to attract—your ideal clients or target market. As you write your initial list of adjectives and labels, search for words those clients would use to describe themselves. I am not wild about age ranges, but that could be part of it. Investable assets, as we discussed, offer you no value. People just don't walk around thinking to themselves, "I am a person with half a million in the bank." You almost certainly will write a number of things down that are too general to be useful on their own, but note them anyway. It's a place where you can start. *Preretiree* and *professional* come to mind. When words like this appear on your list, consider how you could narrow them down. "Preretirees with school-aged children" and "self-employed professionals" are heading in the right direction.

Think about your current client base. Are there any themes running through the list? Are there similarities in career, stage of life, faith community, hobbies, or interests? I discussed that some advisors provide solutions and others provide experiences. If you provide a certain set of solutions, the commonalities should be easier to identify. If most of your clients are self-employed or a certain specialty of doctor, for example, it is pretty easy. If you provide an experience, finding the common themes might be considerably trickier. I worked with one advisor who seemed to have very little that tied all his clients together. We puzzled over what was unique about him and about that group for some time before he accidentally blurted out, "Can I specialize in visual learners?" I asked what he meant. He said that he was very visual and that whenever he brought on a new client, he drew pictures to explain financial concepts. Do you draw pictures for every- thing? I asked. "Pretty much," he replied. It turns out that this is one of the things his clients appreciate most—that he uses illus- trations to make complex concepts understandable. His value proposition became "Personal finances—illustrated."

If you provide more of an experience than a solution, what ties your clients together? What is it about how you do what you do that keeps your clients coming back?

Once you have some initial thoughts about who you believe is your ideal client and what is unique about you, bring it to your client advisory board. When I help an advisor organize a new advisory board, our first agenda almost always includes what I call the *come, stay, and leave questions*. Why did you decide to start working with this advisor in the first place? What is it about what she does that keeps you with her? What is it that she might inadvertently do that would make you leave? These are the questions that will begin the conversation about what your clients find most attractive and most valuable about your practice.

While it might take a couple of meetings, from there you can back into figuring out the description of your ideal client. If you just start out asking clients who they believe is ideal, my experience is that people respond in one of three ways: "Just like me," a stereotypical answer that has nothing to do with themselves or "That's not really for me to decide." If you invite someone to participate on an advisory board because you want more clients like him, the "Just like me" crowd will try to describe someone who is exactly like them. They tend not to do what you need to do, which is to look around at the other people at the table and figure out what they have in common. This is one of the reasons why a good facilitator is so important to a productive advisory board.

More common is the stereotypical answer. Regardless of how you would describe each of the clients you invite, if you ask who the ideal client would be, many people will default to the very attractive and useless descriptors that so many advisors come up with themselves—"Rich," "High income," "With some kind of liquidity event pending," and so on.

Starting out with a discussion of what people find most valuable gives you the opportunity to progress to the question of what other people like them also would find valuable. You can start building a profile of the ideal client as a collection of needs and wants rather than the superficial labels people are likely to think of first. You still may end up with a description that includes career, age range, or life stage, but you start from a more productive place, so you don't necessarily get bogged down in the obvious categories.

Your advisory board is an important partner in this process. Most advisors believe that they know enough about what their clients want to be able to make a list of the most valuable things their clients get from them. However, as I discussed earlier, limiting the conversation to the echo chamber of your own head has some serious problems. I can't remember an advisory board meeting I've been part of where we were not surprised at least once. It might be tempting to skip over this step to save some money and to be able to progress a lot more quickly, but don't. Or if you really want to move so fast that you can't get an advisory board meeting together at this point, don't skip the next opportunity to involve one. In a few paragraphs I will be bringing them back into the process, and that feedback will be even more important.

Once you have a description of your ideal clients, do a little research into what else they may need. If you have had difficulty determining how to differentiate yourself from other advisors, you probably offer all the same things that many other advisors do. Part of what will make you referable is what you can offer your target clients that they cannot find as easily from other advisors. Do some research into your target market. You may find ideas in our trade journals. Depending on the definition of your target market, you may have a population that has its own trade journals or magazines that cater to a common interest. There may be books or research papers focused on a group whose members are similar to your ideal clients.

I must emphasize the importance of looking at topics outside the traditional financial planning space. First, I discussed the issue of differentiation. If you address the same issues and offer the same services as other advisors, it will be very difficult to tell you apart from them. Second, it can be profitable to discover other issues to discuss with clients because it adds value to the relationship. Julie Littlechild concludes from her research[1] that moving clients into the coveted "engaged" category requires having discussions beyond portfolio management. Knowing the topics and issues on your target prospects' minds will help you to understand what kinds of discussions to have outside the investments.

At this point you can begin to envision the future of your practice. Once you have a detailed description of your ideal clients and have done some due diligence on the issues most important to them, you can begin to define the ideal advisors for those clients. What would the practice of a virtuoso advisor look like to your target clients? What kinds of services would it offer? What particular skill set would that advisor have? In many cases I find that an advisor can give a significant boost to her value to clients by adding capabilities. For example, I worked with an advisor who came to define her ideal client as a vice president or higher level of employee of a public company. When we examined that population, we found that there were a number of issues peculiar to that group, including the need to deal with employee stock options and concentrated positions in employer stock. While she had some familiarity with those issues, we realized that a real expertise clearly would differentiate her from other advisors. Once you have identified additional skills that would be valuable to your ideal client, create a learning plan to develop those higher-level capabilities.

TAILORING YOUR STRATEGY

What would your target clients get from an advisory practice that was ideal for them? How does that compare with what your practice looks like today? What changes are you willing to make to bring your practice in line with the ideal? It may turn out that very little needs to be changed. Maybe you just need to learn how to talk about your practice in a different way to communicate its particular value for your target clients. We may find, however, that to be the ideal practice entails some big changes. Consider what changes you would be willing to make.

If you are already successful, you may be resistant to making any significant changes. This is perfectly reasonable. I don't usually recommend too much change too quickly. The fact is that what you have been doing so far has brought you the success you have realized. Changing that in a fundamental way could be analogous to killing the goose that lays the golden eggs. On the other hand, if you are not getting the referrals you want, something needs to change. As Rita Mae Brown paraphrased,[2] simply continuing to do the same things and hoping for a different result is one way to define insanity. Contrary to what you have heard in most referral articles and seminars, simply asking for referrals more often or asking in a better way is not what will get people suddenly remembering to mention you. It's not about what you ask for; it's about who you are and what you do. If you want more referrals, you have to figure out how you are going to change to be more referable. It simply may be changing how you describe what you do. More likely, you will have to make at least a little change in what your practice offers.

At this point you can begin thinking about how you will define your differentiator. Once you have a good, clear vision of what the ideal practice for your target market delivers, how will you describe what makes that practice different from those of other advisors? What solution or experience does your practice deliver that makes it ideal for those particular clients?

But don't change anything yet! So far you have an idea of what your practice can represent, a draft. Before you take any action on it, you need to test it. It's time to go back to the client advisory board.

Explain to your advisory board what you are proposing to change and how you plan to describe it. Make sure that it connects with them. See how enthusiastic they are about it. I have been in meetings where the board embraced new ideas (and subsequently became great referral sources). And I have facilitated meetings where the most valuable advice was not to proceed.

One advisory practice retained me to put together an advisory board to give firm feedback on a service it wanted to introduce having to do with college planning. The advisors were enthusiastic about the service and had a vision of providing advice well beyond the relatively simplistic asset restructuring many advisors offer as a way to maximize financial aid. I asked the group what it would value. I had ideas that included guiding students on selecting an appropriate field of study and matching families with the right educational institutions, in addition to providing advice on the financial aspects of preparing for college. Then I got to pricing. In short, what I learned was that while participants were enthusiastic about discussing the possibilities of what the advisors could offer, almost no one was willing to pay very much to get it. The greatest value I contributed to that process was helping the firm to discover that it should not proceed.

While I believe that it is critical to get client feedback on proposed strategies and services, it is not reasonable or realistic to believe that clients will suggest those new ideas. I don't mean to say that client advisory boards don't come up with some great ideas during their discussions—they do. However, you must take the initiative and come up with interesting ideas to bring to them. You cannot rely on the notion that the board will come up with them. It is one great limitation of client involvement. I heard Lou Harvey, president of Dalbar (the leading financial services market research firm), make this point eloquently in a presentation. After 45 minutes of graphs and charts about innovation and client satisfaction, he came to one of his main points, which was that advisors need to keep bringing ideas to clients to see how they will react to them. The best new ideas will not come from the question, "What else can we do for you?" You cannot simply ask clients what they want, he said, because clients don't know what's possible. Or, as the most famous adage attributed to Henry Ford goes (although he probably never said it[3]), "If you had asked people what they wanted, they would have said faster horses."

Does this mean that gathering client feedback is pointless? No, it means that the kinds of conversations we have with clients need to lead to a deeper understanding of where they want to go, how they want to get there, and the challenges they will face along the way. It is then up to us to translate that into services that will help them along in their journey, which we then can bring back to the clients and ask, "Here, would this help?"

Although they may, and sometimes do, come up with great suggestions of things to investigate, what clients can be relied on to provide to you is an evaluation of how much they value your current services and the ideas that you propose. And this is the feedback you need in order to begin tailoring your strategy and your mix of services to that target population.

BLUE OCEAN STRATEGY

When you make a list of all the things you could do for a client, you will quickly get to a point where it exceeds your ability to deliver on all of it. You may be at that point now, even before you begin this process. Financial plans, recommendations on outside accounts, due diligence on alternative investments, newsletters, appreciation events, following up with accountants and attorneys, tax-lot accounting, loss harvesting, client advisory boards, income projections, employment contract negotiations, guidance on philanthropy—the list could go on just about forever. Your objective is to provide the services your target clients want most. But even that could lead to a list longer than one you could implement profitably. Let me offer a suggestion for one approach that may help you to determine the right balance of things you should try to deliver and things you should not.

This approach comes from *Blue Ocean Strategy*, an article[4] and later a book[5] and an institute created by W. Chan Kim and Renée Mauborgne. Their approach to value innovation helps you to understand how to best use your resources to focus on providing the services your clients want most. Here is an oversimplified approach to the analysis: List all the services you provide as part of your practice. Be specific. If there are separate pieces of your investment management process, list them individually. If your financial planning is delivered in modules, handle them separately rather than simply saying "financial planning." Be thorough. If the people on your staff dedicate any substantial portion of their time to something on a regular basis (even if it's not frequent), make sure that it's on the list.

Show this list to your clients. It would be a great agenda item for a client advisory board meeting. Include it at the end of a review appointment. Send it out as a survey. Find out which of those services your clients consider most valuable and least valuable. Ask them to rate each one on a scale of 1 to 10. Don't ask them to rank them in order—there may be two or three services that rate a 10 and two or three that rate a 2. What you want to find out is what clients think of each one individually.

Then calculate what it takes to deliver each one. You may buy a service, in which case determining cost is easy. It may be strictly a time commitment on the part of yourself or your staff—following up with attorneys or evaluating outside investments. Even preparing financial plans is much more an investment of time than it is in the cost of the planning platform. But do the best you can to evaluate the amount of resources each of those services requires.

Then graph each of those services with value to clients as one axis and cost as the other. An example of what it might look is shown in Figure 10.1. Your graph will not necessarily look like this. In this example, client appreciation events are expensive to provide, but clients do not derive much value from them. In your case, you might find that clients attach a high value to these kinds of events. You may find that clients frequently bring friends to these events and that these friends often become new clients. For this sample practice, the advisor provides individualized client web pages. Clients perceive this as somewhat valuable, and they are moderately expensive to provide. If you provide them, you might find that this is how it

Figure 10.1   Finding the blue ocean—perceived value versus cost.

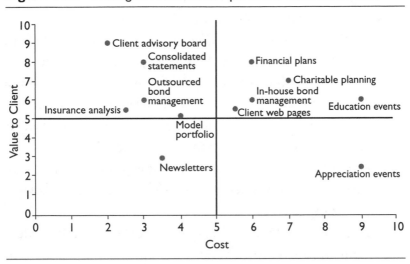

is for you, or you may find that clients find them highly valuable and that they are very inexpensive to provide.

Once you have all the services located on the graph, you are in a position to evaluate the merits of keeping or enhancing the services you provide. In the upper left corner of the graph are the services to which clients attach a high value and that are relatively inexpensive to provide. These are the services you really want to focus on. In the lower right corner of the graph are the services from which clients do not derive much benefit and that are expensive to provide. These are the services you will want to eliminate. Services that are expensive to deliver but create significant value for clients, in the upper right corner, are candidates for analysis. You definitely want to keep them, but it may be worthwhile to investigate ways of doing them more efficiently. Services in the lower left quadrant, not particularly valuable to clients but not expensive to provide, are your call.

Whether or not to hold client events is one example of a discovery the Advisor Impact staff helped to make for an advisor. He had been hosting both client education events and client appreciation events. When he hired Advisor Impact to do a client survey for him, he asked clients how valuable they found each type of event. The feedback he received was that clients loved the education events, appreciated what they learned at them, and often brought friends. The social events, on the other hand, were considered somewhat enjoyable but not at all important. "You just saved me $30,000," he said to the Advisor Impact staff.

You can include in the surveys and on this graph services you intend to offer or different ways of providing services. In this example, the advisor offers customized portfolios of individual bonds to income-oriented retired clients. She is considering outsourcing the management of that program rather than researching and obtaining the bonds in-house, as she has been doing up until now. You can see on the graph that clients find this offering pretty valuable and that outsourcing the service would move the program into a more favorable quadrant. Had she evaluated it and found that the cost savings were not that much, it would not have been worth investigating any further whether to send it out of house. Had we found that the service did not rank highly with clients, she probably would have discontinued offering it altogether.

While I suspect that many practices will employ this analysis to make some minor alterations, fully embracing the idea and a willingness to go wherever your clients' preferences take you potentially could result in a radical new design for your business. To illustrate, let me describe briefly where the Blue Ocean Strategy idea came from.

Kim and Mauborgne were approached by the operator of a circus seeking help in rebuilding a struggling company in what was, and still is, a declining industry. After performing the analysis I just described, they made some interesting discoveries. It turned out that what people liked most about the circus was the tents, the clowns, and the acrobats. Circuses traditionally promoted "stars," but most people did not consider even the most famous circus performers stars in the way they usually used the term. And circus goers were less and less interested in the animal acts because of the growing publicity about their treatment and living conditions. This was great news for the circus owner because the animals and stars were the most expensive parts of his shows, and clowns and acrobats were considerably less expensive. The shows were reorganized around a glitzier tent, more sophisticated acts for the clowns, and a greater focus on acrobatics, and the animal acts were eliminated. What they came up with was Cirque du Soleil, whose productions have been seen by more than 40 million people in 90 countries, generating gross revenues in 20 years equivalent to what it took Ringling Brothers and Barnum & Bailey more than 100 years to attain. If you are willing to be open-minded and take your practice where your clients most want you to go, you may end up with something radically different and wildly successful.

YOUR COMMUNICATION STRATEGY

Once you have refined your service mix and have clarified what your target clients want most and consider most valuable, it's time to figure out how you will communicate your message to the world. Develop your value proposition and long and short versions of your elevator speech. Train your staff to describe your ideal clients and to articulate the special value you represent. Teach your staff, your clients, and your centers of influence the trigger phrases that will help them to recognize an ideal client and the fact that they need what you provide. Incorporate this message into your new employee orientation program, and discuss it or review case studies periodically at staff meetings.

Determine how you will have the new referral conversation with your clients. Script it and rehearse it. Develop a checklist you can use in preparing for client meetings to discover who that client can introduce you to and how you will bring it up in conversation at the end of the meeting. Make a list of other advisors you can refer prospects to when they do not meet your target criteria. Practice the conversation you will have with a prospect when you refer her to another advisor and with your client when you let him know who you sent his referral to. Make sure that those conversations reinforce a description of your ideal client and the unique value you represent.

Update your marketing materials to reflect your new value proposition. (Don't forget to get the reaction of your client advisory board before you commit to your printer or web designer.) Develop a strategy for how you will get this message out on a regular basis—on your blog, in articles, or through public appearances. Discuss with your marketing agency or public-relations consultant your ideal clients and value proposition. Do whatever you can to make sure that when anyone discusses your firm in public, he or she is discussing your unique service offering and your target market.

Identify other kinds of advisors who cater to that same market. Network with them. Get to know their practices so that you know the right people to refer to them.

You can download worksheets to help you organize all these activities at my website: www.theclientdrivenpractice.com/worksheets.

NOW TAKE ACTION!

Succeeding in any business requires that you stand out from the crowd. And the more distinct and special your reputation, the easier it is to attract more clients. So many of the businesses held out to us as examples of the kind of service we should offer (e.g., Ritz-Carlton, Neiman Marcus) embody the concept of not just being better than their competition but providing a separate kind of experience from other companies in their industries.

Standing out in the financial services business is even more of a challenge because for so many of us what we do for clients doesn't just look or sound like what other advisors provide, it actually *is* the same as what other advisors provide. There are probably a lot of other professionals in your town who use the same asset management program, financial planning platform, wealth-reporting system, or website provider as you do. Ultimately, however, you need to find a way to be different.

Maybe it doesn't have to be this way. You could be the one who develops a new way to do things, provides services other advisors haven't thought of, and offers a custom-made experience designed especially for your target clients. People will end up talking about you because what they experienced when they met you was different from what they got from any other financial professional. Your reputation will spread as word gets around that within your professional niche, you are the *one* to go see.

Where can that take you? What rewards and experiences are down that road? The best clients and the best employees are attracted to a leader, someone with vision. Get together with your best clients and paint the picture of what could be. Draw the map and start the journey, and people will follow. Begin the journey. Innovate. Show your clients a new landscape. Bring them something they haven't seen before, something exciting, and they will talk about you. More people will find you.

What will be the first thing you will do? Commit to it today. Take the first step.

I have worked with enough advisors to know that this can be an exciting trip. If I am lucky enough to meet you along the road, I can't wait to hear the stories of where you have been and what you have seen. Good luck and Godspeed!

NOTES

Chapter 1

1. http://www.advisorone.com/2010/12/28/whats-working-or-not.
2. http://www.billgood.com/resources/research/articleviewer.cfm?
   &str_publicationID=804.
3. Ibid.
4. Abraham H. Maslow, *The Psychology of Science*. 1966, p. 15.
5. You can obtain Julie's study at her website: http://www
   .advisorimpact.com/ussite/economics_of_loyalty.html.
6. John Jantsch. *The Referral Engine: Teaching Your Business to
   Market Itself*. New York, NY: Penguin, 2010.
7. http://www.fa-mag.com/online-extras/6470-getting-referrals
   -without-asking.html.

Chapter 2

1. John Jantsch. *The Referral Engine: Teaching Your Business to
   Market Itself*. New York, NY: Penguin, 2010.
2. Scott Degraffenreid and Donna Blandford. *Embracing the
   N.u.d.e. Model—The New Art and Science of Referral Marketing*.
   Scott Degraffenreid and Donna Blandford, 2005.

3. Mark Sisson. *The Primal Blueprint*. Malibu, CA: Primal Nutrition, Inc., 2009.

4. http://www.advisorimpact.com/ussite/economics_of_loyalty .html.

5. Ibid.

6. http://www.ducttapemarketing.com/blog/2009/01/14/seth -godin-thinks-youre-boring/.

7. Paul McCord. "Why Clients Resist Giving Quality Referrals." http://www.isnare.com/?aid=116605&ca=Marketing.

8. https://www.memberlink.net/webfm_send/101.

9. http://www.nsresearch.com/; also described in the article at http://www.financial-planning.com/news/loyalty-wealthy -investors-2672291-1.html.

Chapter 3

1. http://www.advisorimpact.com/ussite/economics_of_loyalty .html.

2. http://www.advisorpod.com/PB037.

3. http://www.kitces.com/blog/archives/121-Why-All -Professionals-Should-Eventually-Have-A-Niche.html.

4. Cerulli Associates. *The Cerulli Edge Advisor Edition*. Phoenix Marketing International. Second Quarter, 2011, p. 3.

5. Seth Godin and Kim Zetter. TED Interview: Tribes Author Says People, Not Ads, Build Social Networks. *Wired*. February 4, 2009. http://www.wired.com/business/2009/02/ted-seth -godin/.

6. http://www.fainsight.com/growthbydesign.html.

7. http://www.advisorone.com/2011/07/28/define-conquer marketing-strategically-to-achieve?page=2.

8. http://www.kitces.com/blog/archives/183-People-Who-Can -Afford-My-Services-Is-NOT-A-Target-Market!.html.

Chapter 4

1. http://www.advisorimpact.com/ussite/economics_of_loyalty.html.
2. Quantitative Update: Advisor Metrics. Cerulli Associates, January 2012.
3. Jaynie L. Smith. *Creating Competitive Advantage*. New York, NY: Doubleday, 2006, p. 100.
4. Eric T. Bradlow, Keith E. Niedermeier, and Patti Williams. *Marketing for Financial Advisors*. New York, NY: McGraw-Hill, 2009.
5. Cerulli Associates. *The Cerulli Edge Advisor Edition*. Phoenix Marketing International. Second Quarter, 2011, p. 7.
6. 2011 U.S. Full Service Investor Satisfaction Study[SM], J.D. Power and Associates, June 2011.
7. "Despite Efforts to Legislate Greater Accountability of Financial Advisors, Consumers Understanding of the Differences Between Fiduciary and Suitability Standards Is Low," J. D. Power Associates Press Release, June 16, 2011.
8. http://sethgodin.typepad.com/seths_blog/2011/11/your -competitive-advantage.html.
9. Scott Ginsberg. *How To Be That Guy*. HELLO, my name is Scott!, 2006.
10. Jaynie L. Smith, *Creating Competitive Advantage*. New York, NY: Doubleday, 2006, p. 21.
11. Jaynie L. Smith. *Creating Competitive Advantage*, New York, NY: Doubleday, 2006, p. 139.

Chapter 5

1. Personal video interview during the winter of 2010 to 2011.
2. Julie Littlechild. *Economics of Loyalty—Anatomy of the Referral*. San Francisco, CA: Charles Schwab & Co, 2010.

3. http://www.advisorone.com/2011/05/09/wealthy-investors-say
   -theyre-happier-with-their-ad.
4. Both Sides Now: Perceptions of the Advisor-Investor
   Relationship, Institute for Private Investors, 2011, https://
   www.memberlink.net/webfm_send/101.
5. http://www.seic.com/enUS/about/5428.htm.
6. Susan Scott. *Fierce Conversations*. New York, NY: The Berkley
   Publishing Group, 2002, pp. 5–6.
7. http://www.kitces.com/blog/archives/144-Its-Not-Just-About
   -Telling-Clients-What-To-Do,-Its-About-Motivating-Them
   -To-Do-It!.html.
8. Personal video interview during the winter of 2010 to 2011.
9. Personal video interview during the winter of 2010 to 2011.
10. Personal video interview during the winter of 2010 to 2011.
11. Personal video interview during the winter of 2010 to 2011.
12. Personal video interview during the winter of 2010 to 2011.
13. Personal video interview during the winter of 2010 to 2011.
14. Personal video interview during the winter of 2010 to 2011.

Chapter 6

1. Julie Littlechild. *Economics of Loyalty—Anatomy of the Referral*.
   San Francisco, CA: Charles Schwab & Co, 2010, p. 6.

Chapter 7

1. www.financial-planning.com/fp_issues/2010_5/david_yeske
   -2666629-1.html.
2. Julie Littlechild. *Economics of Loyalty—Anatomy of the Referral*.
   San Francisco, CA: Charles Schwab & Co, 2010, pp. 25–26.

3. David Meerman Scott. *World Wide Rave: Creating Triggers that Get Millions of People to Spread Your Ideas and Share Your Stories.* Kindle edition. Hoboken, NJ: Wiley, 2009.

4. Scott Degraffenreid and Donna Blandford. *Embracing the N.u.d.e. Model—The New Art and Science of Referral Marketing.* Scott Degraffenreid and Donna Blandford, 2005, p. 63.

5. Gallea, Anthony, *The Lump Sum Handbook*, Prentice Hall, 1994.

Chapter 8

1. John Jantsch, *The Referral Engine: Teaching Your Business to Market Itself*, Kindle edition. Hoboken, NJ: Wiley, 2010, p. 100.

2. http://www.advisorimpact.com/ussite/economics_of_loyalty .html.

3. Sam Richter. *Take the Cold Out of Cold Calling.* Edina, MN: Beaver's Pond Press, 2009, p. 188.

4. John Jecker and David Landy. "Liking a Person as a Function of Doing Him a Favor." *Human Relations* 22(4):371–378, 1969.

Chapter 9

1. http://www.fa-mag.com/component/content/article/38 -features/5764-hatching-a-client-recruitment-plan.html.

Chapter 10

1. Julie Littlechild. *Economics of Loyalty—Anatomy of the Referral.* San Francisco, CA: Charles Schwab & Co, 2010, p. 19.

2. http://en.wikiquote.org/wiki/Rita_Mae_Brown.

3. http://blogs.hbr.org/cs/2011/08/henry_ford_never_said_the_ fast.html.

4. http://hbr.org/2004/10/blue-ocean-strategy/ar/1.

5. W. Chan Kim and Renée Mauborgne. *Blue Ocean Strategy: How to Create Uncontested Market Space and Make Competition Irrelevant.* Boston: Harvard Business Review Press, 2005.

INDEX

ABOUT THE AUTHOR

Stephen Wershing, CFP® coaches financial advisors to engage their best clients in driving the strategic plan of their practices. His firm, The Client Driven Practice, teaches advisors how to focus their business on what clients value most, resulting in elevated productivity, higher profitability, and dramatically increased referrals. He consults with firms on various practice management issues including referral marketing, client advisory boards, improving systems and implementing technology.

He entered the investment and financial planning industry in 1987. His most recent executive positions include President of Ensemble Financial Services from 2002–2010, and Chief Operating Officer of Wall Street Financial Group from 1998–2002.

Steve has authored articles for the Journal of Financial Planning on referrals and client advisory boards, and Financial Advisor on referral marketing. He has been quoted in many trade and popular publications, including *Financial Planning, Investment Advisor, Financial Advisor, Investment News, On Wall Street,* CNBC.com, and *USA Today*. In addition to his own blog, he is a blogger for Advisors4Advisors.com and financial-planning.com. He has presented to industry groups including many chapters of the Financial Planning Association, FPA Business Solutions 2011, the Investment Advisor Magazine Wealth Advisor Summit, and the Business and Wealth Management Conference presented by Bob Veres & T3.

He served as President of the Financial Planning Association of Greater Rochester, NY. He is a Trustee of the Susan B. Anthony House, a member of the Board of Directors of the Hochstein School of Music and Dance, and sits on the Corporate Advisory Council of Flower City Habitat for Humanity. He is on the Editorial Advisory Board of Advisor Products, Inc.